The Winning Spirit

Achieving Olympic Level Performance in Business & Personal Advancement

Edited by
Robert B. Sommer

Griffin Publishing
Torrance, California

10 9 8 7 6 5 4 3

ISBN 1-882180-58-5

PUBLISHER   Griffin Publishing
PRESIDENT   Robert M. Howland

SERIES EDITOR   Richard D. Burns, Ph.D.
COORDINATOR   Robin L. Howland
EDITORIAL   Freda Yoshioka
BOOK DESIGN   Mark M. Dodge

Griffin Publishing and Best of the Masters wish to thank the many other talented and devoted supporters of the Olympic Games who made this publication possible.

For more information about the authors in this publication, please contact Best of the Masters.

Additional Olympic-related materials are available from Griffin Publishing.

Griffin Publishing   **Best of the Masters**
2908 Oregon Court, Ste. I-5   366B El Camino Real
Torrance, California 90503   Encinitas, CA 92024
Phone: (310) 381-0485/ Fax: (310) 381-0499   Phone: (800) 356-3338
                                                 e-mail: RBSommer@aol.com

Manufactured in the United States of America

FOREWORD

When the "Dream Team" was assembled for the 1992 Olympics, every basketball fan loved the prospect of seeing Michael Jordan, Magic Johnson, Larry Bird, Patrick Ewing and Charles Barkley on the floor together. Yet, many sportswriters doubted it would work. Each man was the "franchise player" and the unqualified star of his respective team. Leaders all, but would they be inclined to leave well-fed egos and the habit of personal expectations at home? Could they gel as one force, one unit of excellence? Resoundingly, yes. They did. With ease.

The skeptics had overlooked that before good players become superstars, before they smile and sign their names to sneaker contracts, athletes have to hone some skills. In basketball, these skills start with ball control, no-look passes, driving to the baseline, and a full array of shots. Just as essential, though, to winning consistently enough to get to the championship, they have to learn team play.

This aspect of T*E*A*M (that Together Everyone Accomplishes More) is the seed of Team Pride. It melds individual excellence into team dominance. It did it for the Dream Team, and it is the starting point for every team win. Whatever the sport, whatever the league, whether the NBA, the NFL, the MLB, the NHL, Little League, "Pop" Warner or the Olympics, and whatever the workplace, team wins begin with T*E*A*M-ing.

There are other critical aspects for team wins, of course. A few that come quickly to mind are determining realistic performance goals, curtailing the inevitable creep of inconsequential detail that can misdirect effort, ensuring an atmosphere in which innovation and problem-solving are valued, for instance; but none of these follow-on aspects will be effective until T*E*A*M-ing is both the practical mode and the true emotional spirit of each individual on the team.

You will learn more about team pride in *The Winning Spirit*, and how to marshal your individual talents and accountability to make you team ready. You will meet fascinating individuals and real-life stories that inspire and compel. The project, the brainchild of Rob Sommer at Best of the Masters, was eagerly undertaken by each of the authors appearing here because of their personal interest in and knowledge of what it takes to win at sports, work and in life.

Each author brings an individual perspective and emphasis. Whether you start at the beginning and read through to the end, or skip around to areas that interest you the most, there is much to discover in *The Winning Spirit*, and all of it can be put into immediate effect.

As a concluding note, on behalf of everyone involved in *The Winning Spirit*, I would like to give a salute to the American Olympians headed to Atlanta in 1996. There is no greater success in athletics than to be an Olympian. That dream has fueled them through literally hundreds of hours of training. They go to Atlanta with our respect and pride.

Congratulations to each of them, and to their coaches, trainers, parents, loved ones and all the millions of Americans who volunteer their time and give their support to the Olympic Committee.

Jim Tunney, Ed.D.
Pebble Beach, California
October 14, 1995

CONTENTS

Part One: Internal Processes

Part Two: In Training

Part Three: People and Winning Examples

INTRODUCTION

Robert B. Sommer, Editor

When asked about my favorite wish or dream, the answer has always been…to be a member of a U.S. Olympic team.

Many of us probably share this same dream as we watch the magnificence of the Olympic Games on television and marvel at the flawless execution of gymnastic routines and the incredible speeds and heights achieved on the track. From our living rooms, we vicariously share the athlete's sense of fulfillment as he or she becomes the first to cross the finish line or achieves the highest score. The personal sense of achievement that athletes must feel when they are successful as Olympians is a feeling that we would all like to experience.

While relatively few of us have the talent to become an Olympic athlete, we can, however, aspire to perform at Olympic standards.

In my association with successful people from many walks of life— sports, business, and academia—I've concluded that the secret to success is an Olympic-style dedication to a goal. This involves mental and physical discipline, ideals and desire.

This book represents the thoughts of twenty of the nation's leading counselors in the search for success. Take advantage of their insights and guidance to create your own Olympic experience and to discover *The Winning Spirit*. Phone: 800-356-3338; e-mail; RBSommer@aol.com.

1

OLYMPIC THINKING

by Bill Bachrach

Bill Bachrach is speaker, author and consultant exclusively to the financial services industry. A former retail financial advisor, his book, *Values-Based Selling: The Art of Building High-Trust Client Relationships*, is the only industry-specific resource of its kind and establishes standards for financial advisors and insurance agents. He is president of San Diego-based Bachrach & Associates. Phone: 800-347-3707

If your profession were an Olympic event, would you make the team? If you made the team, would you win a medal? Can you imagine what it would be like to feel the weight of the gold medal on the center of your chest while your flag is being raised to the sound of your national anthem? You can have similar feelings in your personal and professional life if you adopt what I call "Olympic Thinking."

One reason we admire Olympians is because of their high standards. These high standards are the reason Olympians perform as they do. Raise your own standards, apply some "Olympic Thinking" and improve *your* performance as a result.

OLYMPIC THINKERS TAKE RISKS

At the 1988 Olympic Games in Seoul, Korea, millions of television viewers around the world watched as American gold-medalist Greg Louganis hit his head on the board during the ninth dive of the spring-board preliminaries. Only 12 divers would qualify for the finals. Greg's accident dropped him from first to fifth place. With four stitches in his head and a water-proof patch, Greg returned for his next dive and executed possibly the best dive of the competition. Everyone watching witnessed this moment of extraordinary courage. In his book, *Breaking the Silence*, Greg said, "You don't win gold medals by playing it safe."

In our business and personal lives we can't play it safe and expect to achieve our highest levels of success. Fortunately, the risks are seldom as severe as we imagine and the rewards are often greater than we expect. If the primary motivation behind your decisions is to avoid unlikely worst-case scenarios, your options will be severely restricted. Olympic thinkers take risks and don't permit the remote possibility of negative results to overshadow the probable positive results.

OLYMPIC THINKERS DON'T MAKE EXCUSES

Olympians with high standards seldom make excuses. Having a good excuse for a poor performance does not compare with the feeling of accomplishment that comes with producing results. Olympic thinkers focus on results.

Having a good excuse for missing your children's special events is not as good as being there. Having a good reason for not meeting your sales goals is not the same as achieving them. Having a good excuse for not taking care of your physical health is not the same as being physically fit. Failing with an excuse is simply not as good as succeeding.

"Only the best practice when they don't feel like it or when it is inconvenient," says Olympic gold medalist Peter Vidmar. "To make the Olympic team, I had to be an even higher achiever. I made a clear list of objectives that I had to accomplish every day in the gym. If my workout lasted three hours, great! If the workout lasted six hours, tough luck! I wouldn't leave without accomplishing my objectives. My daily goal was to leave knowing that I had done everything I could." Olympic thinkers focus on results and figure out a way to stay on track with their work program, training program, or their health program.

OLYMPIC THINKERS EXPRESS THEIR GREATNESS

There are many ways to express who we are. Olympic athletes express themselves and maximize their talent in a physical endeavor. Whether we are salespeople, homemakers, executives, professionals, managers, or administrative staff, we have an obligation (not just to ourselves, but to the people we care about and who care about us)—a commitment—to push ourselves to full capacity. In today's business climate, this is not just the key to success, it may be the key to survival. Maybe it is unreasonable to push ourselves or others to be great in all areas of our lives, but surely it's reasonable to become great at *something*.

My friend Sigurd Dusenberry is a good example of expressing greatness. At age 37, only reasonably active and 15 pounds overweight, Sigurd decided to do a triathlon. In 1983, he completed his first triathlon: a 3/4-mile swim, 20-mile bike ride, and 5-mile run. He struggled to finish that race. But, in October of 1987, at age 41, Sigurd successfully finished the Hawaii Ironman triathlon. The Ironman is the premier triathlon. It's a 2.4-mile swim, followed by a 112-mile bike ride, finishing with a full 26.2-mile marathon, all in the same day. The Ironman doesn't take place in the luxurious, comfortable locations in Hawaii. Instead, it's hot, usually more than 100 degrees, in the lava fields of Kona where the bike race and marathon take place. The 30-mph gusting winds make the biking extremely challenging. Sigurd's goal was to finish in 12 hours. His actual time was 11 hours and 47 minutes.

How did he do it? He committed himself to express his greatness and was consistent in his efforts. Sigurd started his training slowly and consistently raised his standard of performance until he accomplished his ultimate goal: the Ironman. "I literally never missed a workout that was in my training log," according to Sigurd. His commitment to his training schedule was impressive. If he was supposed to ride X miles on Tuesday, he rode X miles on Tuesday. Sigurd stuck to his schedule regardless of the weather or how he felt. What would happen in your business or personal life if everyday, whether you felt like it or not, you did what it takes to express your greatness?

"People are impressed when they find out I finished the Ironman," Sigurd says. "I'm not super-human. Anyone could do it. It's just a question of sticking to your training commitments and putting in the mileage."Olympic thinkers express their greatness by keeping their commitments to themselves and others.

OLYMPIC THINKERS, CHANGE AND CHALLENGE

Olympic thinkers respond positively to change and challenge. Consider Steve Jobs and Steve Wosniak, founders of Apple Computer. They didn't start Apple just to help people be more efficient, they wanted to *revolutionize* people's lives. Their team banded together to change the world. Their blue jeans and tee-shirt culture focused on results, not convention. Their purpose drove them to perform extraordinarily well. When they needed someone to help them take the Macintosh computer from the drawing board to the marketplace, they didn't use money or prestige to lure John Sculley, a respected marketing "genius," away from Pepsi-Cola. Sculley already had a seven-figure compensation package and plenty of prestige at Pepsi. Why would he change careers? Steve Jobs had spent two years developing a friendship with John Sculley, but had not yet convinced

John to come to Apple Computer. One day, according to Sculley's autobiography (*Odyssey: From Pepsi to Apple—A Journey of Adventure, Ideas, and the Future*), Jobs and Sculley were walking near Sculley's home when Jobs asked, "So, what do you want to do, John? Do you want to sell sugared water for the rest of your life...or do you want a chance to change the world?" In that moment John Sculley knew what he had to do. Jobs' challenge was the turning point. John Sculley gave up his career as President and CEO at Pepsi to move to Apple. He went from a business where he was a legend to an industry he knew nothing about. John Sculley successfully brought the Macintosh computer to the market. Macintosh changed the world and so did John Sculley. Olympic thinkers embrace change and thrive on new challenges.

OLYMPIC THINKERS ATTRACT OTHER OLYMPIC THINKERS

Bart Conner, Olympic gold-medal gymnast, says, "Success breeds success." A workplace with high standards attracts workers with high standards. Even better, the environment with high standards *repels* people with low standards. Conversely, an environment with low standards also repels people with high standards. Managers who want to attract capable producers with track records of personal and business success have to ask themselves tough questions about the work environment they have created:

• Why would a highly qualified person come to work for you?

• Does your office display substantial evidence of success?

• Are your standards significantly higher than the industry averages?

• Does your environment support successful people or people who are struggling?

• How many of your emloyees have actually achieved the incomes, leisure time, recognition, and quality of life referred to during recruiting?

Ironically, some managers don't even realize their standards are low. A successful second-year financial advisor was overheard discussing the standards in his office. He said, "I was proud of my accomplishment of being hired here. During my interviews, I had the impression that only the best would be selected. I thought that not performing up to the established standards would mean termination. I was motivated to be successful and I expected to be surrounded by others who felt the same way. Now that I've been here a couple of years, I realize our company will hire and keep just about anybody."

A successful high-standards environment becomes a "recruiting magnet" because more successful people are attracted to it. Bart Conner is correct: Success breeds success. It's a great cycle that only a handful of managers and organizations ever experience. You have to pay more than lip service to high standards because successful people see through the "talk" if you don't "walk the walk." How does this apply to your environment?

Salespeople with high standards attract better clients. Managers with high standards attract better staff. Business owners with high standards attract better employees. Leaders with high standards attract better subordinates. Companies with high standards attract better executives. It makes perfect sense. Olympic thinkers reward success, therefore they get more of it.

OLYMPIC THINKERS TEND TO BE PERFECTIONISTS

It's an interesting paradox that the same people who criticize their friends or colleagues for being perfectionists can be moved to tears watching an Olympian score a perfect 10 or set a new world record. It's difficult not to appreciate perfection. Olympic thinkers tend to seek perfection. When you compete with the best, what else can you do?

If perfection is not your goal, it is difficult to achieve high levels of success. Would you rather have a goal of a perfect 10 and fall short with a 9.9 or set your goal at 8 and achieve it? The Olympic thinker prefers the better *result*. Beware of using perfectionism as an excuse to fail or not produce results: Remember, Olympic thinkers produce results, not excuses. Seeking perfection doesn't mean you never get things done. It means you get things done well.

Nadia Comaneci was the first Olympic gymnast to score a perfect 10. During an interview, Comaneci explained, "I always underestimated what I did by saying 'I can do better.' To be an Olympic champion you have to be a little abnormal and work harder than everyone else.

Being normal is not great because you will have a boring life. I live by a code I created: Don't pray for an easy life, pray to be a strong person." Olympic thinkers seek perfection as their ultimate goal.

THE PROBLEM WITH HIGH STANDARDS

Olympic thinkers recognize that the problem with high standards is that most people choose not to have them. So when you choose high standards you choose to be in the minority. Olympic thinkers would rather be in the high-standards minority rather than the mediocre majority.

Those who choose mediocre standards have a large support group. Those who choose high standards discover a *real* support group. Mediocre people "support" each other by buying each other's excuses and letting one another off the hook. The people with high standards truly support one another with encouragement to take their endeavors to the highest levels possible. For example, the mediocre leader, coach, or manager will tell you to set "attainable" goals, which usually means setting goals too low. Leaders with high standards urge you to set high goals that might seem unattainable and then help you stretch to attain them. Which do you think is more satisfying?

Perhaps people set their standards low to avoid failure. Yet, you are much more likely to fail because your standards are too low, not because they are too high. In fact, can you think of people or companies who failed because their standards were too high? Neither can I. But it's easy to think of people and companies who failed because their standards were too low.

People with high standards always set the new standard. Having just won two gold medals in Lillehammer, Norway, at the 1994 Winter Olympics, Bonnie Blair did not go home to gather endorsement contracts or be the guest of honor in the parades. Instead, she made a classic high-standards, Olympic-thinker trip to Calgary. Her collection of five Olympic gold medals (the most won by any U.S. female Olympian) would have been enough for most, but Bonnie Blair was in the best speed-skating condition of her life and she had one more challenge to meet. No female speed skater had ever gone faster than 39 seconds in the 500 meters, so Blair went to the Olympic Oval Finale Invitational event in Calgary to see if she could break this barrier. When she crossed the finish line in 38.99 seconds, she became the first woman to break this barrier. Blair's world record was to women's speed skating what Roger Bannister's first sub-4-minute mile in 1954 was to running. One year later, at the World Cup in Calgary, Blair beat her own world record for the 500 meters in 38.69 seconds.

Why is Bonnie Blair one of the greatest Olympians in history? She epitomizes the high-standards Olympian. She is an example for all of us who aspire to be Olympic thinkers. You can't choose mediocrity and be an Olympic thinker.

OLYMPIC THINKERS SEEK FEEDBACK

Do you look for ways to do your job better? Do you seek constructive input? Are you always seeking a higher level? People with high standards seek feedback.

Tom Olivo is president of Success Profiles, a company dedicated to measuring an organization's performance in comparison to *best* practices (not the average). Tom says, "research has shown that you can only learn about 30 percent of what you need to know about your customers from normal business interaction. The other 70 percent must come from research known as feedback."

As a salesperson you can seek feedback from your customers, your leaders, and other top salespeople about the quality of your prospect interviews and sales presentations. Some of your best feedback will come from role-playing on video tape and audio taping client interactions. These tapes can be uncomfortable to watch and listen to at first, but they provide an incredible opportunity for growth. Leaders can solicit feedback from subordinates, customers, and other respected executives. Every person with high standards can find a way to get feedback. If you can't find a source of feedback for free, hire it. It will quickly pay for itself.

Feedback serves as the measurement system for improvement. Feedback sets the benchmarks for achieving the high standards you have set for yourself.

Norman Vincent Peale once said, "Unfortunately most people would rather be ruined by praise than saved by criticism." This doesn't mean you have to subject yourself to abuse. It does mean you should seek feedback from people who will tell you the truth, not just make you feel good. Olympic thinkers seek feedback and welcome input to improve.

OLYMPIC THINKERS WORK SMART

Being your best is not about being a workaholic. Athletes learn to get the most out of their bodies with the least amount of stress. Training used to be hammer, hammer, hammer. Now training is a balance of intensity, light workouts, *rest*, and nutrition. It has become an art and science, not just work. Much has been discovered about the relationship between time off and improved performance.

The same is true in business and sales. The objective is results, not hours worked. No matter how much you enjoy your work, your work is only a single component of a full life. And a full life is the foundation of a high quality of life. Your work is the financial fuel for the rest of your life as well as *one* source of personal satisfaction.

By being really good, you can spend far less time working and still produce exceptional results. Just be sure to focus on work that rewards you for your results, not just the hours you work. Even in this era of downsizing, people who produce results are in demand.

Olympic thinkers look for the most effective, least time-consuming ways to produce their results so they enjoy the best quality of life.

WHY BECOME AN OLYMPIC THINKER?

Having the high standards of the Olympic thinker will enable you to enjoy life's tangible rewards. But, more directly, high standards will impact your total quality of life and how you feel about yourself. Be an Olympic Thinker. Raise your standards and your performance will improve directly.

2

MENTAL BICEPS

by Jim Tunney, Ed.D., C.S.P., C.P.A.E

As one of the NFL's most respected referees, Jim Tunney worked with such prominent coaches as Tom Landry, John Madden and Vince Lombardi. During his 31 years of experience with championship teams, Tunney learned firsthand the key ingredients of a winning team. As a professional speaker, Tunney's seminars and keynotes focus on motivation, customer service, wellness, leadership, team building and increasing productivity. He blends humor and content to create educational and inspirational programs for today's competitive environment. Phone: 408-649-3200

Making it to the Olympics testifies that practice has won out over distraction during years of preparation. Stiff competition forces fierce concentration. Only those who have the persistence and guts to work hard enough and long enough are still there after the "cuts" are made.

This is true for musicians, dancers, golfers, surgeons and everyone whose talent or skill requires muscular control and mental clarity at the time of performance. Indeed, I have heard concentration defined as just that—*mental clarity.*

Preparation and concentration are no less important in activities that require memory of facts and quick recall (ask any "Jeopardy" player) or when insights must be drawn from a base of technical knowledge and applied to a new situation (ask a medical researcher or trial lawyer). Traditional education trains us in the idea of the mind being able to handle facts and draw understandings from them, so we tend to give less credit to everyday mental marvels than we do to physical feats. Maybe that's because muscles hurt when they are stretched and made stronger and brains don't.

You say, "What? I've been mentally tired."

Probably. But the description is askew. Operated by electrical and neuro-chemical transmissions, our brains do not experience fatigue in the same way as do our muscles and general body system. In serious cases of injury, illness, malnutrition, extended fasting, or sleep deprivation, the brain may not get the oxygen and fuel it needs to work properly, or be overwhelmed by fluid or pressure, or have its own form of electrical storms or transformer explosions, but those events are the result of trauma, abuse or neglect, not fatigue. Mostly what we mean when we say we are "mentally tired," is that we're bored, or resentful, or temporarily or chronically undercommitted, not "brain dead." Our emotions give out, not our minds.

IN TRAINING FOR MENTAL CLARITY
That distinction aside, in both muscular and factual memory, training provides the foundation for the mental clarity, the relaxed

concentration, which produces the self-confident, trusting effort that allows the muscular precision and power, or the quick recall and instant insight, that proves the preparation and makes the performance.

Take a quarterback, under pressure and about to get sacked, yet who manages to get off a bullet that spirals 60 yards and connects just where he aims it. Touchdown! Or consider a pianist playing the presto movement in Chopin's B-flat Minor Sonata. In doing either, there isn't time to think—only to do. So, what's going on that we're not aware of? How do we manage the quick and complex mind-to-muscle communication that happens faster than thought?

I've never played Chopin, or any piano. Neither have I learned to type or knit, each a skill requiring finger dexterity and kinetic (muscular) memory. I have never thrown a 60-yard bullet under pressure either, but by tossing shorter passes, dribbling a basketball and slamming an occasional home run, and refereeing more than 500 NFL games, I have learned the importance of the distinction Vince Lombardi made when he said, "Practice doesn't make perfect; *perfect* practice makes perfect."

But, you say, if our conscious minds cannot process the muscular information necessary to play the piano, type, knit, pass, dribble or hit as fast as the event happens in performance, how do we reach for perfection in something we can't think fast enough to do?

The answer is simple, and a paradox. Just do it. The mind will take care of the muscles if you take care of the mind. Your job at the conscious level is to hold your mind aware, trusting, focused and relaxed simultaneously, without fret, without worry, but aware, until the muscles take over on their own. Your job is to be there without getting in the way. At the unconscious level, a lot more is going on.

Take that presto movement in Chopin's B-flat Minor Sonata. And why not invite Mozart into the room as well. Remember that scene in the movie *Amadeus*, when Mozart is dismissed by the king with the rebuke, "Too many notes." The king's ears couldn't keep up with Mozart's fingers. Chopin must have loved Mozart, for in Chopin's presto there are 1,760 notes to be played in one minute 16 seconds flat. That's 23 notes per second!

Most people, even accomplished musicians, cannot scan 23 notes per second (hitting the limits of conscious mental processing again), much less move each of ten fingers up, down and sideways, getting two fingers out of the way for each one that makes a correct strike, at the speed of 23 strikes per second according to an arbitrary pattern (the idea is to play Chopin as he wrote it, after all) and do it flawlessly 76 times in a row.

That feat, strung out in words or tinkled out on the piano, makes connecting on a 60-yard touchdown pass sound mundane, but what it takes to do either, indeed, what it takes to do all feats requiring kinetic competence, requires the same thing: *ballistic* training, careful, patient practice with the small involuntary muscles.

BALLISTIC MOVEMENTS

As the name suggests, ballistic movements are like firing a gun. Once the bullet leaves, it's on its way and will go where it was aimed. If you know where it started, its force and trajectory, you can reliably predict where it will strike.

It's the same with ballistic muscle movement. Once a small electrical release is given, just enough spark to set the direction and speed, the muscle follows through. Like a bullet, the muscle continues on its path until its force is used up or hits resistance. The brain controls only the initial signal, which requires much less time than the full movement.

That's the secret. Once the signal is sent, the brain is free to manage the next signal, moving quickly on. In this way, the brain can orchestrate a chorus of activity for the involuntary muscles in a small amount of time. It needs only about 80 milliseconds to aim and fire each signal.

Large muscles are "wired" differently. The brain uses continuous-feedback signals to correct direction and amount of force for them. This is why we can be adaptive—jump back when startled, switch direction, change speed, stay balanced in a rowboat, adjust the face of a tennis racquet to compensate for more or less topspin on a return of a serve, and signally handle all the movements of the voluntary muscles in close to real-time signally from the time of decision to act.

ADAPTIVE MOVEMENTS

The flexibility and adaptiveness of voluntary muscle control give us gracefulness (some more than others, me not much). Because ballistic movements are unchangeable once triggered, we would have awkward, robot-like movements if they were the only form of mind-to-muscle communication. Adaptive movements also give us the effectiveness of choice, but what they offer in effectiveness they sacrifice in efficiency. The continuous-feedback signal needed for adaptive movement requires something around 400 milliseconds per action, or about five times more processing time than ballistic movements.

Through practice, we can develop speed and reliability in both adaptive or ballistic movements, but you can see now why training must be specific and consistent, "aimed" toward "perfection" in small muscle training.

The maxim in coaching is that if you want to change the performance, you have to change the training. This is thoroughly true in ballistic movement training. If you do not train perfectly to the goal, the training does no good. In fact, inconsistent or haphazard effort is more than a waste of time; it can actually erode the effectiveness of earlier strict attention. The mind can't set the pattern for aiming the signals, proving Lombardi's critical distinction. Practice doesn't make perfect. Perfect practice makes perfect.

PRACTICE PERFECTLY

No one I've known in sports was more insistent on perfect execution than Lombardi. Any highlight film of Lombardi's years at the Green Bay Packers during the 1960s includes a wild-eyed Lombardi barking to the hapless player who just blew a play, "That's not how the Green Bay Packers do it. If you're going execute like that you're not going to be a Green Bay Packer!" Lombardi is mythologized for having boasted to an opposing coach, "I'll give you my playbook and we'll still win, because we'll execute better than you can defend against us." We're talking total confidence here.

Lombardi said his winning teams were built on four principles: self-discipline, self-sacrifice, mental toughness, and teamwork. He recognized that without all four elements, he couldn't reasonably count on his players to focus hard enough and long enough to out-execute the opponent in any circumstance, and that's what makes a winner.

He liked to win. More than that, Lombardi hated to lose, and because he believed in his formula, he tolerated no slack from his players. He coached hard to get what he wanted and he expected his players to want it hard. Lombardi knew that each player had to win the head fight; individually, each player had to be victor over his own uncertainties and the confusion and distractions that deflect attention before he could be valuable in making the team victorious. Conviction is a private experience, self-made.

But there's a difference between the kind of focus and commitment that Lombardi talked about and everyday "hard work." It has become popular to consider anyone who "works hard" as a "workaholic," and therefore a candidate for an early heart attack, stress-related diseases, etc. This assumption is mistaken. Hard work isn't stressful; working hard without seeing positive results is stressful. Stress doesn't kill you, *dis*tress may. This is part of the difference between mere tenacity and what Lombardi meant by *mental toughness*.

MENTAL TOUGHNESS

You may have the determination to stay at something, to keep trying, to never give up, but mental toughness means you also have the self-control and focus to limit your efforts to only the ones that are effective.

Take the guy who wants to get out of debt so he decides to trade his Porsche for a BMW instead of accepting his uncle's offer to inherit the family Chevy. You may hear the guy moaning about "hard choices," but he didn't make the one that would get real results. He didn't have the "toughness" to commit.

Take tennis as another example. Anyone who wants to get really good at tennis has the same goal: not to lose more than two points in a row. If you never lose two points in a row, you will never lose a game or a match. Sounds simple, right? Trouble is, to play that tightly, that perfectly, you have to keep constant focus on the narrowest goal that will assure success.

The ability to concentrate powerfully and continually carve away distraction and ineffective action is the essence of Lombardi's mental toughness. It is the power to focus forcefully and "do it right the first time, every time."

When the competition matters, whether it's the Buffalo Bills against the Miami Dolphins, or unpaid bills against dollars not in the bank, the "winners" will be the "toughest" ones, the ones willing to make the hard choices of conviction and stay committed to the narrowest goal that will assure success.

DAILY HEROICS

There is an element of courage mixed in here with this discussion about conviction and commitment. A central attribute of courage is the ability to perform in spite of tension or fear, to be able to concentrate and execute just as skillfully and deliberately in a tight spot as in ordinary circumstances. We generally think of courage in terms of physical feats, and we tend to idolize physical courage. We make instant heroes out of people who brave war, confront a mugger on the street, run into burning buildings to save a life and all such heroics. That kind of fear is palpable.

Yet, most of the ways we are called upon to be courageous are in facing emotional and mental challenges, not physical ones. Career shifts, downsizing, factory closings, office politics, rebellious children, errant, inattentive or insensitive spouses, traffic jams, dented fenders, technological bewilderment, our nation's widening apathy counterpointed with polarized anger and divisiveness. These and their thousand cousins are the "threats" we face every day, and we rarely earn hero status for surviving them.

What training or skill is there for increasing your ability to persevere through muddles and hassles without losing the doer's energy?

What inspires the commitment to huddle-up and stay focused on the narrowest goal to assure success? What fosters the self-reliance it takes to tackle something new, to keep learning continuous and willingness proactive instead of price-controlled? What mental glue binds hardiness with patience to make tenacity, and then laminates that tenacity with discipline to form mental toughness?

I don't know, exactly, but that quality, that strength I call courage is threaded throughout our efforts to achieve higher levels of excellence.

What is courage? I don't know that either, exactly. Sometimes we can see a situation better from reverse angle (like they do on television with instant replay in slo-mo). If we look at what courage is not, we can say with some forcefulness that courageous actions are never rash, ruthless, sneaky, impetuous, blind, or unimportant.

And we can say positively that when being courageous, actions are internally decided and do not come from bosses, coaches, sergeants or peers. Courage, too, is a private experience, self-made.

GOAL-SETTING MACHINES

Most of literature and our experience takes us to the conclusion that humans are at their best when facing a challenge, even adversity. People innately seek to stretch themselves.

They naturally set goals. Indeed, the mind is a virtual goal-setting machine. It is not accidental that the state-of-mind we call happiness occurs when a live connection exists between our sense of ourselves and our sense of purpose. This state, in all its shadings—satisfaction, optimism, and eagerness—includes every moment of solution or decision.

Unfortunately the mental and emotional abilities that create happiness can, when misdirected or left to drift, unaimed, just as powerfully undermine and erode our sense of purpose and sense of ourselves. You might assume that detouring into indecision or a funk is the path of least resistance. However, it takes as much energy to struggle to your defeat as it takes to surmount whatever is necessary to achieve your goals (if you use your intelligence and potential effectively and wisely) because despair and frustration are more self-absorbing and the obsession lasts longer than joy and satisfaction. This is natural and good. Why? A certain restlessness has been built into us. I'm not referring here to the primal and violent survival mechanisms, such as protecting territory. Most of our survival techniques are much more subtle, and useful.

Take curiosity. It's the genesis of many goals, and goals themselves are one of the features that defines human intelligence. It takes abstract thinking to form a goal, to envision the future, to create an image of what we want. Then, in a confrontation with ourselves—a showdown in the mind, really—we consider both the facts and our feelings. Out of this mental stew comes a conclusion, a goal, and through this process we determine if we use our powers beneficially and to the maximum, or if, in effect, we defeat ourselves.

TACKLING YOURSELF

How often has it seemed that you were in some situation, about to take action, and then messed it up without any real interference, except from yourself? Even with clear vision, we can trip ourselves. This is what I call "tackling yourself." We all are good at it. It is bound to happen, unless and until you teach yourself not to do it.

To be in charge of your life, you must first be in charge of yourself. We all face continual frustration because we can't control the events and circumstances around us. It's reasonable, even inevitable, because individuals cannot hope to control the complex network of people and nature that comprises our lives. But we can improve our self-control and become less vulnerable to common frustrations and self-imposed defeats. It's summed up in the phrase, "Get hold of yourself."

Now, the thing to notice is that this increase in self-control involves the same dynamics as goal-setting. They are both simply the result of mental sifting. You sort through the problem, list your resources and the possibilities, and in doing this you either set your resolve and concentration, or you become bogged down in confusion and indecision. Every test of life, like Lombardi's game readiness, is first a head fight, interior and singular.

Commitment, like its buddies conviction and courage, is a private experience, self-made.

What we often do in dealing with ourselves is bind ourselves in, not spring ourselves out. We listen to an internal pessimist, to the might nots, instead of the mights and wills. We develop cycles of thought and reaction patterns—habits of mind, really—that tend to create downward spirals of mood. This breeds confusion and depression. It reduces emotional energy instead of increasing it. Ennui, a fatigue of the spirit, ensues.

Much of "feeling down" results from trying to do so much that we must continually accommodate frustration and disappointment. This reflects our modern misplaced emphasis on outcome. Center your focus on two things: the goal (your choice) and the process used toward it (again, your choice). The outcome of the effort is actually immaterial to happiness and the prospect of future success.

If you set a realistic goal and intelligently, powerfully seek it, you will have demonstrated self-control, conviction, and courage. And when you add in what you learned, your "failure" becomes, at worst, only temporary. The assessment of why and how you "failed" will lead to a new, more carefully crafted goal. Let me have Lombardi say it again straight, "Perfection may be impossible; excellence is not."

SKIP THE SAG AND LAG

Next time you are getting down on yourself or life, notice that a setback leads to the next goal as naturally as success does. The trouble is the lagtime. It costs so much time and energy. All is lost between the judgment that it was a "failure," and the reassertion of will to move on. This lagtime is a time and spirit waster. Skip it, or at least practice shortening the sag and lag.

The action, the movement, the power, the growth, the satisfaction are found in "going for it"—in making the choice of the goal and then striving. As Jerry Rice said, "Ya gotta strive before you thrive." When Rice, the record-breaking surefire future Hall of Fame wide receiver for the San Francisco 49ers, who maybe the hardest worker in the NFL, shows up early for training camp and every practice, he is in his striving mode. His goal is firmly set as he stretches, sprints, sweats and hones his skills, many of which are ballistic movements.

There are no records to be broken on the practice field. That opportunity comes on game day, but Rice knows, as Lombardi knew and all winners come to understand, that you don't execute in game conditions unless you practice toward perfection, intently and with the same mental toughness you want to have on game day. If you want to change the performance, change the training, and mental training comes before physical training. Rice not only shows up early physically. He shows up mentally ready, focused, committed, willing to make the hard choices of doing only what is effective and doing it long enough and hard enough to improve, so that what he wants to do under pressure he can do without thinking.

This kind of mental toughness, this self-control, this commitment, courage and conviction involves both mental attention and emotional responsibility. It demands that you keep your spirit taut and engaged. There's no time for rest, yet you experience less fatigue than those who are not trying as hard. It's a paradox, a marvelous skill for sports, and all the more important in real life.

3

How to Be Your Own Olympic Coach

by Bill Brooks, CSP, CPAE

A former college football coach and president of a national 300-million dollar sales organization, Bill Brooks is the author of seven books, hundreds of audio and video programs, as well as software sales tools. His materials are used worldwide to enhance sales success in organizations of all sizes and his clients include General Motors, Hewlett-Packard, Borden's Dairies, Isuzu and Mack Trucks. He holds a master's degree from Syracuse University. Phines: 800-633-7762 336-282-6303; e-mail: Bill@thebrooksgroup.com; web site: www.brooksgroup.com.

Even the very best of Olympic competitors cannot become champions without help. In the rough and tumble world of world-class competition there is a single, common factor that all performers share. Champions and also-rans alike all have coaches whose purpose is to teach, inspire, reinforce, cajole and constantly demand the best from their willing pupils.

In both our personal and professional lives we, too, need coaches. Lots of organizations work diligently to develop leaders, managers, supervisors and the like. Unfortunately, far too little time and effort is invested in developing coaches.

As a consequence, many people are forced to become their own coaches. Required to strike out and "make it or break it" on their own, people must use their own resources while they simultaneously develop their own plans for personal and professional growth.

What is it that a coach is really expected to do? Let's take a look at seven very specific and key functions:

- Establish expectations
- Create a motivational environment
- Develop strategies and tactics
- Teach and train
- Reinforce success patterns
- Measure results and course correct as necessary
- Establish new expectations

These functions of coaching are actually components of the Cycle of Coaching Success. This cycle is just as applicable to a sales, manufacturing or service organization as it is to an Olympic, collegiate or professional athletic team. A coach must...

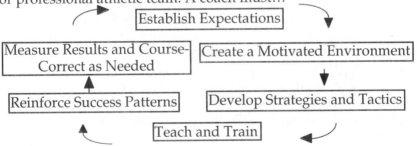

The path to any success is through a continuously evolving cycle of development. The coach cultivates the cycle of development that ends where it begins, only with improved and significantly higher levels of expectations, skills and success patterns.

Now that the function of the coach has been defined, the next question is, "How can one become his or her own coach?" It's pretty simple. The first thing to do is simply to decide that you are willing to do it, that you are committed to assuming full responsibility for your own actions, results and performances.

In today's highly competitive world it has become increasingly more evident that ultimately, your own success and security depend on your ability to perform, not upon any organization or group of people, but on *your* ability to perform. Ultimately, your success and security depend on your coaching yourself to higher levels of performance. Knowing precisely how to coach yourself is what this article is all about.

I was in an airport recently talking with a highly successful business executive. He was relating to me how he belonged to various business, religious, personal and professional support groups. He confided in me that he depended on all these support systems since he secretly lacked the self-confidence, discipline and ability to withstand the diversions and temptations in his life.

In an indirect way, he had accepted the role of being his own Performance Coach by engaging a series of assistant coaches to help him. Accepting ultimate, personal control of your own destiny is an inside game, and a highly individual one. Not one for others to do, the game is strictly up to you.

There will probably come a time, though, when the above executive must be willing to face the darkness alone. During the Civil War, soldiers used the phrase "seeing the elephant" to define the harrowing experience of combat. In hand-to-hand combat (or one-on-one sales, crisis management or "seeing your own elephant," no matter what it is), there comes a time when you will have to reach within and use your very best skills without the help of others to bring out the best you have to offer. That is really becoming your own coach.

COACH'S FIRST RESPONSIBILITY

Having decided to become your own coach, certain preliminary duties are in order. The first of these is to define your core competencies. In the case of Olympic athletes, they must define their competitive event. Long-distance runners certainly have a set of talents different from sprinters, and swimmers from basketball players, just as salespeople have different competencies from managers, and entrepreneurs from corporate executives.

What is your talent? Perhaps just as important, what do you really care passionately about? What do you want to do more than anything else in the world (even if you are not paid to do it)? Nothing great was ever achieved without talent being intimately linked to passion. Nothing is more frustrating than passion without talent and nothing more wasteful than talent without emotional commitment.

The greatest coaches of all are the ones who can identify talent, place that talent in the right situation and then fuel their players' or participants' inner passions. You have to do the same thing for yourself. No guru, management expert, support group, consultant or counselor can do that for you. Only you, and you alone, are in the position to do it for yourself. Others may help you along the way, but ultimately, it is up to you.

BEGIN THE COACHING CYCLE

Once you have identified your talent and fixed your emotional eye on the target you must clearly define the long-term goals you want to achieve and begin the Cycle of Coaching Success. What do you want to be? Olympians are ultimate goal seekers. For some it may be to represent their countries well, for others it may be to become a part of the team. For others it is to be a medal winner. Some are aiming only at the gold.

In defining your goals, you have to anticipate how will you feel when you achieve your goal. How will you even know when you achieve it? With an Olympic athlete the goal is very clear. It is defined for them. Win or lose. Make the team or not. Beat a certain time. Earn a medal or not. In the other areas of our lives where we are setting goals, the delineation is not so clear. Therefore, it is up to you to define in very clear terms what victory means for you, not for anyone else.

Will victory mean that your family can achieve a certain lifestyle? Or, perhaps surviving as a nuclear family is your goal. Becoming financially independent; working because you want to, not because you have to; establishing a good, solid reputation as a professional; achieving worldwide fame are various career goals. How about your personal gold medal? Do you want a medal for changing the world or more modestly, for raising healthy, productive children?

The bottom line is this: In the areas of your life that really matter, how will you ultimately define victory? Without clear definition there can never be any clear victory. And unclear victory leads to lingering doubt, frustration and anguish. Athletic competition provides a unambiguous, black and white definition of success. Perhaps that is why we admire athletic competition so very much. There is no confusion about success. You have the winners and the also-rans. In life, it is not so clear.

Practice, feedback, practice

In order to coach ourselves to victory we have to go to the next step. We have defined our talent, tapped into a strong passion for doing it, clarified our target or measurement for defining victory and now we must simultaneously accomplish two things in our dual role as both trainee and coach:

- Continually refine our skills through repetitive practice, and,
- Learn from both positive and negative feedback.

These two aspects go hand-in-hand. In the final analysis, the biggest challenge to being your own coach is obtaining an accurate self-perception. Self-limiting behavior, blind spots as to how we really perform and a lack of clear self-perception are all deterrents to the self-coach.

A good coach can videotape a performance or simply observe activity and suggest immediate correction. That is a very tough thing to do when you are evaluating your own performance. Consequently, a good, solid objective baseline analysis plays an essential part in one's ability to self-coach. In short, without a baseline measurement of current performance, it is impossible to determine what to practice and what to improve.

Once an objective analysis is made, the next step is to learn through both positive *and* negative feedback. The Law of Effect states simply that behaviors that are reinforced are most likely to be repeated.

If you talk to most athletes they will tell you that they rely on videotaped replay to study their successful patterns of performance. They will also tell you that through studying their errors, they learn what to eliminate. Frankly, seeing is believing.

Returning to the Cycle of Coaching Success, let's take a look at each step in more detail.

ESTABLISHING EXPECTATIONS

What do you really want to accomplish? What can you realistically expect to achieve in your career, your life? Realistic expectations lead to a meaningful, fruitful and profitable sense of self-direction. Unrealistic expectations can dash your hopes through the frustration of unfulfilled dreams and a gnawing sense of frustration.

CREATING A MOTIVATIONAL ENVIRONMENT

This responsibility has perhaps the most options for self-coaching. Every single one of us always has the right to choose. Whether we are making mundane choices such as what to have for a meal or momentous choices such as the type of job or profession we pursue, we all have choices. Deciding what environment to be in and how to create it or respond to it are both very personal choices and very important ones.

DEVELOPING STRATEGIES AND TACTICS

The world is filled with people who have lofty goals but who never seem to do things that drive them toward the fulfillment of their dreams. Coaches are great at developing overall tactics, strategies and related skill sets for their athletes. In the absence of external coaches, though, we must constantly strive to ensure we are doing the right things for the right reasons…and at the right times.

How do we do that? By dogged and diligent study, by constant self-improvement, by becoming a real student of our profession or vocation, by observing the best and mirroring their behavior and by being willing to put it all on the line. Test and fail. Test and succeed.

TEACHING AND TRAINING

Like the previous step, this step also requires dogged commitment. It also demands that constant attention be paid to day-to-day, step-by-step skill improvement, sometimes to the point of tedium.

Having a correctly defined strategy for success is one thing (a career path or professional development strategy), but doggedly honing the skills to make it happen is something else entirely.

A salesperson who never gets better at closing sales or qualifying buyers will soon fail no matter what his or her career aspirations in sales might be. A business owner who never becomes financially literate could easily fail—and fail fast—without learning how to read financial statements.

The bottom line is this: It is up to you to learn the necessary skills to become more proficient at whatever it is you want to undertake. Formal or informal training programs, seminars, tapes, books, videos, home study courses and the like abound. In today's Information Age there is absolutely no excuse for failing to master skills, except for one…laziness.

REINFORCING SUCCESS PATTERNS

This one is easy. Simply repeat those behaviors and activities that have produced successful results and don't repeat those behaviors that have proven to be less successful. Coaches spend lots of time having athletes repeat their success patterns, from successful basketball shots to powerful pole vaults and high jumps.

What have you been most successful in doing in the past? Repeat every pattern that led you to that success—feel it, think about it, act it out beforehand in your mind, then mentally replay that success scenario over and over in your mind before, during and after the next event. It makes no difference at all whether that event is a sale, an interpersonal relationship or even a physical activity. You will be amazed at how powerful visualizing your success pattern and then actually doing it will be for you.

MEASURING RESULTS AND COURSE CORRECTING

In athletic events, scores are kept. There are stop watches, tape measures, winners and losers. If a person is afraid to face these truths, then head-to-head athletic competition is no place for that person to be.

Leading a fulfilling and meaningful life is the same. If a person is either unwilling or unable to face the results of their efforts, then perhaps that lifestyle is not the best choice.

Be willing to be measured. And measure yourself against your goals. You win or you lose. Sound harsh? Athletic competition is harsh too, isn't it? Some athletes will get the gold. Others will go home disappointed. Some of those who go home disappointed will come back to win the Olympics in four years. They are the few who will learn from their results and course correct as needed. Can you do the same thing? More specifically, are you willing to do the same thing?

ESTABLISHING NEW EXPECTATIONS

The best coaches are those who can take athletes to the "next level." This is also true of the best managers, leaders, supervisors and organizers of any group of people. It is also true of the best self-coaches. They are capable of taking themselves to new, higher and more demanding levels of performance. Setting new standards...expecting and achieving more. It is meeting the challenges of the game that separates the Olympic champion from the rest of the pack. Meeting the challenges of life will separate you from the rest of the pack, too.

There are clear choices open to everyone. There is one choice that no one can really afford to avoid: the choice to become your own coach.

4

THE DYNAMICS OF
OLYMPIC MOTIVATION

by Don Hutson, CSP, CPAE

Don Hutson has been teaching professional salesmanship for more than 25 years and has addressed more than two-thirds of the Fortune 500. He stresses the secrets of building value rather than cutting price. The author of *The Sale*, his areas of expertise include sales success, customer service, leadership, vision and peak performance.

Wꜱhat percentage of our potential do we tap on a daily basis to perform our jobs? Behavioral scientists say we normally summon only 16 to 18 percent of our total potential. I am convinced that exceptional performers access a consistently higher amount but this is difficult to quantify. Performance experts agree that no one functions at full capacity and we all have significant room for improvement. So…what determines whether we choose to grow and progress or not? I believe growth and improvement depend on the source and intensity of our motivation.

MOTIVATION…HYPE OR SUBSTANCE?

The word *motivation* has a negative connotation to some people. On a recent flight, I was talking with my seat mate who, after I told him I was a motivational speaker, promptly told me that motivation was of no value because it doesn't last. I assured him that the benefits of a bath don't either but it's still a good idea to take one once in a while!

With the people who say that motivation is only a temporary, hyped condition, I take issue. When we are motivated to action, our adrenaline flows and the fire in the belly gets turned up, inspiring us to take aggressive and immediate actions toward the achievement of our goals. When conducting a seminar recently, I had an audience member ask me, "How long does hype last?" I didn't know the answer. Does hype last for two minutes, two hours, two days, two weeks, two months or two years? After considerable consideration, I concluded that the answer to the question was not nearly as important as the decisions that we make and the actions that we take while we are motivated. We are the sum total of the decisions we've made, and when we make a decision, we are doing something which can alter the course of our productive life.

DIRECTION AND INTENSITY

The degree to which an individual strives to achieve greater things, in my estimation, is determined by the direction and intensity of his or her motivation. *Direction* is determined by the quality of decisions made and actions taken. *Intensity* is determined by the fire in the belly, the passion, with which we approach the task.

People with positive direction and high intensity of motivation are self-starters. They don't wander around, looking for someone to fire them up because they're already motivated. Self-starters have internalized their motivation and are accountable for their own behavioral results. Knowing what turns us on enables us to plug into that source of power effectively and often. This is the means by which we successfully internalize our motivation.

DEFINING MOTIVATION

P. T. Young defined motivation as "…the process of arousing activity, maintaining the activity in progress, and regulating the pattern of activity." Activity is obviously the focus in this definition. Motivation within the human tends to generate activity toward the creation of our desired outcomes. I believe the greater the intensity of the focus on our desired outcomes, the more effectively directed our activities will be.

The highest achievers invariably get the most done in a given time-frame because of this focused intensity. They have a mission and they will not be denied. They don't say, "I will achieve my goal if things go okay." And it's a good thing they don't say this because circumstances change. High-achievers must stay focused in the midst of any ambiguity.

Bob Bale defined motivation as "…an idea, emotion or need from within a person which incites that person to act or not to act." The most important words in that definition are *from within a person*. I'm convinced that, ultimately, all motivation is self-motivation. People make happen what they decide to make happen. Therefore, the quality of our decisions is vitally important.

THE POWER OF VISION

So many people are so locked into their habit structure that decisions to take new, productive actions become very difficult to make. Vow to broaden your horizons with new exciting visions and goals; expand your range of skills; push the envelope with energized new behavior and refreshing new approaches to achievement. Listen to tapes; read books; and eagerly try new ideas.

Extraordinary producers in any field demonstrate what I think we could refer to as Olympic Motivation. You don't see athletes who have earned the right to compete in the Olympics who had only goals of "pretty good" performance! They were inspired to develop visions of exceptional, even record-breaking performance. These people don't just push the envelope, they destroy it! They consistently set new standards for themselves and others through the power of vividly imagined visions of positive results.

Dr. Peter Drucker said "the best way to predict your future is to create it!" Have you got the courage to do it, or will you, like most people succumb to behavior by habit...reliving yesterday over and over?

John Sculley, author of *Odyssey: Pepsi to Apple—A Journey of Adventure, Ideas, and the Future,* was quoted in the *Wall Street Journal* recently as having said, "The individuals and organizations busily performing the policies, procedures and habits of the past rather than focusing on visions and opportunities of the future will not be among the survivors!" We must develop and pursue the process of continually re-engineering ourselves to seize opportunities as they appear.

Another quote I love about vision is from my friend, Jerry Bresser, who said, "There are no unrealistic goals; there are only unrealistic time-frames!" This thought has been an inspiration to me for many years. The obvious implication is that we can be motivated to achieve anything if we give ourselves a reasonable time frame. The next subtopic will tell you how to capitalize on the power of vision.

A SHORT COURSE IN SELF-IMAGE

To effectively re-engineer yourself and your behavior for higher achievement, become a student of your own behavioral processes. This will entail an inventory and analysis of all of your strengths and weaknesses. I suggest you consult four sources of input for your lists: yourself and three other people who know you well and whose opinions you respect.

Once you've compiled your comprehensive lists of strengths and weaknesses, go to work on a proactive game plan to do two critical things: 1) Build the foundation for future success on your carefully identified strengths; and, 2) Do all you consciously can to eliminate your weaknesses and any behaviors which are slowing down your achievement process. For those weaknesses you have difficulty eliminating, at least figure out a way to manage them so that they don't significantly get in your way. It's hard to run a race or compete in business if you are dragging balls and chains from your legs.

THE BASICS OF GOAL SETTING

The single greatest problem with the goal-setting process is that people don't attach enough seriousness to it. A recent survey revealed that only one half of one percent of the American work force had their goals in writing! Don't commit that sin—you'll be doomed to mediocrity in most competitive fields.

As your goals and visions start to come together, get serious about them! Remember the advice of Jim Rohn, "Work from document, not just from thought."

I recommend a goal-setting procedure which encompasses eight simple categories: Career, Education/Personal Development, Family, Financial, Physical, Social/Hobbies, Spiritual, and Miscellaneous. I have found that just about any type of goal can be logically put into one of these categories. Think, too, about the critical issue of time allotted for goal achievement.

When you start to put your goals in writing, things begin to take a new and more significant meaning. I tell people..."Be careful what you write down, because it is probably going to happen!"

THE LATITUDE OF YOUR ATTITUDE

You have always heard that your attitude makes the difference. I concur! When it comes to being an internally motivated high achiever, attitude is a crucial element. I'll bet in the first chapter of the first self-help book you read many years ago, you were exposed to a philosophy that went like this..."Whether you think you can or you think you can't, you're right!"

In this world, there are winners and there are whiners. Have you noticed that you seldom hear highly successful whining? You know who the whiners are: they cheer everyone up when they leave the room. They come to work with their own personal clouds hovering over their heads. Their first order of the day is to moan and groan about any negative topic they deem handy to pounce upon and eventually try to get you to join them under their cloud. Don't do it! The whiners usually end up in a self-pity mode, which I recommend you avoid at all costs.

Most psychologists will tell you that many forms of mental illness are derived from thought patterns of self-pity. I recommend you decide now to never participate in that emotion. It is counterproductive to successful behavior and consistently high levels of personal motivation.

DEALING WITH INTERRUPTIVE ELEMENTS

Have you noticed in your quest for Olympic performance that things do not always go perfectly?! More often than not, plans get interrupted by unexpected obstacles and visions are made hazy by unanticipated barriers to results.

The question is not, "Will you encounter obstacles and problems on the way to goal achievement?" You undoubtedly will. The question is "How will you handle the obstacles, problems and ambiguities that rear their ugly heads at the worst of times?" Your resilience will be one of the most critical issues. Will you stay focused and motivated even in the presence of interruptive elements?

In my opinion, you must vow when the goal is set to charge ahead even in the midst of adversities.

THE PEAKS AND VALLEYS OF PERFORMANCE

The highest achievers are those who, over time, are able to heighten their peaks and make their periodic valleys shallower. In charting their performances over a given time frame, you will also observe that their overall trend line is upward. Consistent progress and the upgrading of performance earmark high-achiever behavior.

If valleys become an issue, remember that everyone periodically experiences a slump. The key is to recognize it, analyze it, and get out of it as soon as is practical. One way to assure productive slump-reactive behavior is to maintain a healthy, positive, can-do attitude.

Never gravitate into the depths of self-pity. Nothing will doom you more quickly!

The real winners are always trying to push the envelope toward new peaks of performance. They are energized by reaching new levels of productivity and heights of excellence. They are endlessly tweaking every aspect of their success process, trying to pry another 1 percent of improvement out of themselves.

Don't be discouraged by the valleys, be encouraged by every opportunity for improvement. Always be thinking about motivation toward betterment.

I hope as you read this chapter (indeed, this book) you will be inclined to make some positive decisions. Books can and do change lives to the degree that open-minded readers glean ideas, make decisions and take action. Be among the proud minority with the courage to make a move! Don't ever forget that Olympic Performance is always preceded by Olympic Motivation!

5

THE ART OF
SELF-MOTIVATION

by Bonnie St. John Deane

Bonnie has motivated herself to win Olympic ski medals, a Rhodes Scholarship, degrees from Harvard and Oxford, and praise as a White House official. She balances a career in international marketing and finance with marriage and motherhood. Bonnie teaches corporations and associations self-motivation skills, emphasizing achievement and managing change with less burnout. Phone: 619-558-1105; e-mail: getahead@sjd.com, web site: www.sjd.com.

Growing up in hospitals, in leg-braces, and on the wrong side of the tracks, didn't stop me from believing that an African-American girl with only one leg could learn to ski. And as soon as I did learn to ski a little, I set my sights on qualifying to compete in the 1984 Disabled Olympics in Innsbruck, Austria. Such a big dream, such an outrageous dream, made me stand taller just thinking about it.

My big break came when an elite ski academy in Vermont accepted me as a student. For three months I searched for grants, scholarships, and sponsors to no avail. I will never forget the moment when I told the headmaster I couldn't afford the tuition and I had failed to find sponsors. He said, "Come anyway." I knew this opportunity would change my life.

And then it happened. On the first day of school at Burke Mountain Academy, I broke my leg—my real leg—while playing on a skateboard.

As the only kid there with one leg, I had so badly wanted to show them I could run obstacle courses, jump rope, and play soccer. Instead, walking on crutches with my artificial leg I could barely get from my room to dinner without tripping on stones in the path. Being so thoroughly inept among a crowd of super athletes hurt more than my injuries. At night I cried in my pillow to keep my roommate from hearing.

Although the doctor removed my cast after six weeks, my luck did not improve. Less than a week out of the cast, my artificial leg broke in half. When you think things can't get any worse, you're wrong. For three weeks my prosthesis roamed the country, lost in the U.S. Postal Service.

Years later, standing on the winner's platform in Innsbruck, Austria, as the silver medal was hung around my neck, I could hear the National Anthem playing and see the Stars and Stripes fluttering behind me in the frosty night air. Dreams of that moment had pulled me through all the tough times. Do you have a powerful dream that captures your heart and picks you up when you fall down?

Telling stories like this one was how I began inspirational speaking more than 10 years ago. And there would always be one person in the audience who would come up to me afterwards, grab my arm and ask, eyes demanding, "You motivate others so well, but what motivates *you*?" At a loss in the face of such desperation, I searched for an answer. I read and reread books on positive thinking, psychology, management, and inspirational systems. Finally, when the answer came, its simplicity made me laugh: *I motivate me.*

In this chapter you will learn the world's easiest, most reliable system for motivating yourself. Anyone can complete the five exercises in this chapter in less than one hour and get the key to start his or her own engine. This is the best thing I have ever learned.

Anyone who manages people needs this system for developing more super-achievers. "The difference between people who exercise initiative and those who don't is literally the difference between night and day," says Stephen Covey, author of *Seven Habits of Highly Effective People*. "I'm not talking about 25 to 50 percent difference in effectiveness; I'm talking about a 5000-plus percent difference."

Herman Cain, CEO of Godfather Pizza, argues that self-motivation is the only way to stay competitive. "Nobody motivates today's workers," he says emphatically. " If it doesn't come from within, it doesn't come." Unfortunately, most managers treat self-motivation simply as a skill an employee has or doesn't have. Most managers don't have a system for teaching employees to motivate themselves. Until now.

CORE CONCEPTS OF THE MOTIVATION METER SYSTEM

In a nutshell: Would you walk six miles for a million dollars?

Most people say they would. Would you do it in the rain? Barefoot? "It might take all night," said one woman in my workshop, "but I would do it."

If, instead of one million dollars, I offered you a ticket in the California lottery, would you still walk six miles barefoot in the rain? No? Not even if the jackpot were $16 million? Your decision illustrates the basic mechanism of motivation.

Every one of us is capable of instantaneously making a complex calculation about our motivation to act. Without even realizing it, everyone automatically estimates:

PAYOFF X ODDS OF SUCCESS - WORK = *MOTIVATION*

In this chapter you will learn how to take conscious control of the motivation equation in your head...and to teach others to do so as well.

In the example above, the payoff changed from $1 million to $16 million, the odds changed from a sure thing to a lottery ticket, and the work varied from walking six miles to walking barefoot in the rain. Juggling these variables, you instantly computed whether your level of motivation was high or low. You do it all the time.

TV advertisers understand the power of this equation. "Use my diet pills," they say. "You will be more sexy, more loved. It's as easy as popping a pill and it always works!" You may be highly motivated, but are you motivated by *you*?

In half-day workshops, I teach people to take conscious control of their motivation by measuring it with the Motivation Meter System. In this chapter, however, we will bypass the math and focus on the three basic concepts.

For any project or goal you are working on, you can increase your motivation by: 1) finding bigger payoffs; 2) improving your odds of success; and 3) reducing the work required. Although these ideas seem like common sense, few people apply them systematically to adjust their motivation.

Please stop now and complete Exercise 1 carefully on a separate sheet of paper. You'll want to keep your answers handy for Exercises 2 through 5.

EXERCISE 1: WHAT ARE YOUR PAYOFFS?

Step 1—Spend five minutes listing everything you have ever wanted to have in your life: new clothes, vacations, ideal relationships, peak experiences, career accomplishments, etc.

Step 2—Circle an item on the list which you never actually get around to doing anything about.

BIGGER PAYOFFS AND HIGHER MOTIVATION

Payoffs, in the Motivation Meter System, are more than money. Money payoffs represent the means to things like expensive cars or bigger houses. Nonmonetary rewards, like a job you love or more time with family, can also be payoffs. In all cases, "things" are less important than what those things *mean* to you personally.

Payoffs are highly individual. "The only vision that motivates you is your vision," says William O'Brien, President of Hanover Insurance. Peter Senge, author of *The Fifth Discipline: The Art of the Learning Organization*, puts it another way: "Organizations intent on building shared visions continually encourage members to develop their personal visions."

Making personal payoffs bigger doesn't necessarily entail getting more things or setting higher goals. Bigger payoffs are those which have more meaning for you. Everyone searches for meaning in their lives.

Do you know a person who agonizes, prays to or consults gurus, asking about the Meaning of Life? I imagine God up in the sky shaking his head and thinking, "I made this magnificent creature, put him into a world so full of mystery and beauty that he could spend a lifetime studying a simple thing like water, and what does he do? He asks me about the meaning of life! Each of you has the entire world as your canvas. Don't ask me what to do. I'm curious to see what each of you, as unique individuals, as my penultimate creation, can create. Do something meaningful to you!"

Take a look at the list of dreams you made in Exercise 1. Star items that excite you. Using the dream you circled earlier (the item which you never actually get around to doing anything about), complete Exercise 2.

EXERCISE 2: FINDING THE DEEPER MEANING IN YOUR GOALS

Step 1—For the goal or dream you selected in Exercise 1 (or any goal), ask yourself, What's in it for you? Why do you want it?

Step 2—For whatever answer you wrote above…why do you want that?

Step 3—Keep digging underneath your goals to find personally compelling reasons. Dig down to find out what you really want out of life. Like a little child, keep asking yourself, why? Why? WHY?

Step 4—If the final answer is, "I should," or "My boss wants me to," scratch it off your list.

Step 5—If you can't scratch it off but it doesn't excite you, change it. Expand it. Aim higher.

When digging underneath your dream uncovers meaningless results, aim higher. "Be bold," wrote Basil King, "and mighty forces will come to your aid." Similarly, Norman Vincent Peale urged, "Learn to pray big prayers. Prayers have to have suction in them."

Teaching people to make their own payoffs bigger saves managers from the two pitfalls of using the same incentives for everyone and investing lots of time psychoanalyzing the individual motives of each employee.

HOW TO REACH YOUR DREAMS WITH HALF THE WORK...OR LESS!

This is my favorite part of the Motivation Meter System because it feels like cheating. Who wouldn't be more motivated to go after his or her dreams if less work was involved? The first strategy alone, "Two-fers," is guaranteed to cut the work required for your goals in half.

Work Reduction Strategy No. 1: TWO-FER!

Find ways to reach two different goals with one piece of work. Gordon Burgett, author of more than 1500 magazine articles, taught me to research an article thoroughly and then write it from five different slants for five different magazines. You get paid five times for one research session.

Two-fers abound. Doesn't everyone need to be learning new skills and serving the community in some way? Practice leadership, PR or fundraising skills by helping your favorite charity, political organization, or professional association. Want to get more exercise? Create a business networking group that meets at the gym. Review your master list of goals and find other creative ways to get two for the price of one.

Work Reduction Strategy No. 2: Do the hard work!

In sales, doing the hard work may mean preparation and research on your customer's business. A General Instruments sales executive told this story: "I stayed especially close to the customer and came in at 195 percent of quota, tops in my division. A fellow in corporate called me and said, 'Good job to be sure, but you average 1.2 sales calls a day and the company averages 4.6. Just think what you could sell if you could get your average up to par.' You can guess my response after I came down off the ceiling. I said, 'Just think what the rest could sell if they could get their averages down to 1.2!'" Doing the hard work, in this case, spending more time on each customer, yielded more sales in fewer calls.

Work Reduction Strategy No. 3: Work Immediately

Just Do It! Get started. Don't wait until you have all the answers, until you are ready for the hard work or until the moon is full. Do easy little things that fit your schedule, things on the way to something else. When you're ready, all the little things you did smooth the way.

Work Reduction Strategy No. 4: Work Fun

When my mother wants her closets cleaned out, she organizes the garage sale of the Century. The whole block joins together to put up the signs and pay for the newspaper ad. And when people show up, she gets rolling. One prospective buyer made the mistake of asking, "Is that ring a family heirloom?" My lovely African-American mother answered, "Oh yes. My great-grandmother smuggled it over in a banana." She brought down the house. In the end, she makes a little money, gets the neighborhood spirit going, meets new people, and gives the leftovers to a good cause. And, by the way, she gets her closets cleaned out. Find your fun.

If you are a manager, don't insist on the "best way," a.k.a. *your way*. Encourage employees to work with their skills, their personalities, and their styles.

Work Reduction Strategy No. 5: Work Together

I won't belabor this age-old technique for making work easier. Get an exercise buddy, start a support group, or join a professional association.

Work Reduction Strategy No. 6: Work Lovingly

J. Peterman built a catalog clothing business from nothing to $50 million in just six years. His catalog features only one item per page, with a hand-rendered drawing and an intriguing story about how the item was found, who makes it and why you will treasure that item for a lifetime. "Our customers have a love affair with our catalog," says Peterman.

You don't have to wear a white collar to work lovingly, either. One taxi driver in New York city is reputed to earn $30,000 more per year than other cabbies in tips alone. Once underway, he offers passengers a choice of several newspapers, cold drinks, and a basket of fresh fruit. "What kind of music do you like?" he asks. "Classical, Jazz, Rock, or Gospel?" If a cab driver can put so much love into his work, can't you?

Work Reduction Strategy No. 7: Work Effectively

"Do what you love and the money will follow," wrote Marsha Sinetar.

Until then, love what you do. When asked whether he will do whatever it takes to satisfy a customer, Jeff Thompson, CEO of $24-million Peripheral Outlet, answers a resounding "No!" He elaborates, "If a customer's demands are totally out of line and a company capitulates, perhaps losing money in the deal, how can that possibly cement a good relationship?" Put your nose to the grindstone, but first find the right grindstone.

EXERCISE 3: GETTING YOUR DREAMS AT HALF PRICE (OR LESS!)

Step 1—Using your list of goals and dreams from Exercise 1, identify three ways to get "two-fers."

Step 2—Pick one goal and list at least five creative ways to cut the work. If you get stuck, ask a friend to help!

IMPROVE YOUR CHANCES OF SUCCEEDING ON EVERY PROJECT

In Africa a poor farmer spent years struggling to raise crops in rocky soil which was difficult to till. So miserable was he that stories of "easy wealth" seduced him into selling his farm to hunt for diamonds.

For the rest of his life he wandered the vast African continent searching for the gleaming gems so many others had found. But the great discovery always eluded him. Finally, in a fit of despondency, broken financially, spiritually, and emotionally, he threw himself into a river and drowned.

Meanwhile, the man who purchased his farm for a pittance found an unusual stone in a river cutting through the land. It turned out to be a diamond of enormous size. Stunned by his newfound wealth, he learned the property was littered with diamonds, the very rocks making the land difficult to till.

In this true story from Dennis Kimbro's *Think and Grow Rich: A Black Choice*, it was the farmer's *belief* that his land was worthless that made it worthless to him. Do you frequently underestimate your chances for success? Do you have acres of diamonds inside you that you have ignored?

Overestimating the odds, on the other hand, can spur people to tackle monumental tasks…and win! "Entrepreneurs tend to be overly optimistic," concludes Thomas Jones, author of *Entrepreneurism*, after interviewing founders of Avery Labels, Vidal Sassoon, Kentucky Fried Chicken, and other companies. Err on the side of optimism.

EXERCISE 4: ARE YOU A CHRONIC UNDERESTIMATOR OF YOUR ODDS FOR SUCCESS?

Here's how to dramatically improve your motivation:

Step 1—Pick one of the below to do now.

Step 2—Pick another and put it on your calendar now.

1. Think of one way to spend less time around negative people.

2. Decide to smile at people even when they are rude. Why let them ruin your inner attitude in addition to being rude?

3. Think of one way to spend more time around a successful or upbeat person.

4. Obtain and Read (or listen on tape to) one of the following:

Live Your Dreams, Les Brown

Think and Grow Rich: A Black Choice, Dennis Kimbro

Awaken the Giant Within, Anthony Robbins

Do What You Love and the Money Will Follow, Marsha Sinetar

5. Enroll in a health club or start an exercise program

6. Sign up for a workshop on self-esteem, confidence, or positive thinking.

7. Read the rest of this book!

8. List your own ideas for getting your odds guestimates in line with reality.

Don't ever settle for positive thinking techniques alone. Personally, I am so pessimistic, positive thinking won't motivate me unless I also investigate the real odds and work on improving them.

EXERCISE 5: CHANGING YOUR REAL ODDS OF WINNING

Put the odds in your favor; Learn from people who have done it.

Step 1—List your resources.

Step 2—Circle one and act on it.

Step 3—Circle another and put it on your calendar now.

Step 4—Relax! Don't feel you have to do everything on the list. You can get there with books, people or groups. Do what you love!

Congratulations! You have successfully completed the Motivation Meter System course. This Motivation Meter System can help achieve anything that the mind can conceive. My story, for example, doesn't end on the winner's platform at the Olympics. Since then, I have motivated myself to finish degrees from Harvard and Oxford, to win a Rhodes Scholarship, to win awards as an IBM sales representative, and to garner high praise as a White House official on the National Economic Council. Truly, there is no limit.

Share these ideas with your friends, your family, and your children, your coworkers and employees. The Motivation Meter System is the best thing I ever figured out. If you are not afraid of success, learn it, use it, and master it.

6

PATTERNS OF PEAK PERFORMANCE

by Rick Barrera, CSP

With a degree in marketing and an award-winning 15-year sales career that included telemarketing, door-to-door, business-to-business and retail selling, Rick Barrera started his own company for teaching sales techniques. He is dedicated to helping his clients improve their sales results, increase their customer service efforts and redesign their businesses to compete and thrive in today's complex marketplace. His interactive audio, video and print training resources are designed to help businesses improve their relationships with customers. Based in La Jolla, California, he is co-author of *Non-Manipulative Selling*. Phone: 619-759-2559; web site: www.barrera.com.

Have you ever wondered what separates a peak performer from the average person? What makes one person more successful than another? What does an Olympic athlete have that makes him or her that much better than the competitors?

Some may say the difference between Olympic athletes and average people is biological or hereditary. Others claim that people are products of their environment. Some may even say that it's all luck, or being in the right place at the right time.

I've been studying peak performers for more than fifteen years and every peak performer I've studied has displayed three *clearly learnable patterns:*

- The ability to **create a clear picture** of the desired outcome;
- The ability to **keep his or her mind in the here and now;** and
- The ability to **shift focus from the picture to the process** and the actions necessary to make the picture a reality.

Having a clear picture of the desired outcome means setting goals but I'm not referring to material goals like a big house, a million dollars or a fancy car. Those are all fine supplemental goals if they're important to you, but in this discussion of setting goals, I'm talking about goals that will enable you to grow as a human being, to reach beyond *who you are* and what *you are* currently, goals in which you achieve something.

When you look at a true peak performer, such as an Olympic athlete, you'll see someone engaged in a contest. The contest is not with the outside world to beat some objective standard or to be something for someone else. The peak performer is competing internally to become the best that he or she can be at that given moment and for his or her own reasons. Peak performers are driven by what is important to them, not by the external trappings of success.

Sam Walton was the richest man in America, yet he drove an old pickup truck and worked hard at least six days a week. He said that what drove him was the excitement of teaching young people the thrill of serving the public and selling something at a profit. The point is to create your own picture of what success looks like for *you*.

CREATING YOUR OWN PICTURE

The lack of a picture or goal is often the greatest source of stress for many people. It's like running a race with no finish line. You're pouring out all of your energy but there is no end in sight. The result is stress, fatigue and burnout.

I frequently ask people what they would do with their lives if I could wave my magic wand and they could be anything or do anything they choose.

Some of the people I ask have no dream, but when pressed, I find most of them really do have at least an idea of what they would like to do or become. What amazes me is how few have any plans whatsoever for attempting to realize their dreams. What is even more amazing is that most of them have the ability and the resources available to accomplish their dreams, but they don't even try.

Peak performance takes effort and the very first effort is to create in your own mind a crystal clear picture of exactly what you want and what you want to become. In other words, you need a *very clear picture of your desired outcomes*.

At this point, picture one outcome you would like to achieve in your life and ask yourself the following questions:

1. How will I know when I've achieved it?
2. What will it look like?
3. What will it sound like?
4. What will it feel like?

The following anecdote demonstrates why a clear picture is so important and how quickly you can get exceptional results when you have a focused picture.

One of my associates has trouble sleeping when her husband is out of town. She came to work one day and told me she had been up all night because she had heard noises and feared an intruder would attack her. I asked her what she would have done had her husband been with her. She laughed and said that was a good question because her husband doesn't do anything when she reports hearing noises. He says, "It's nothing, go to sleep!"

Then I asked her what she was doing differently since she was alone. She had a whole list. She left lights on in the living room. She left the bedroom door open. She kept the television on to scare away burglars. She slept on his side of the bed facing the door, an arrangement that resulted in her sleeping on her other side.

In other words, what she saw, what she heard and what she felt during her nights of poor sleep performances were all completely different than what she saw, heard and felt in her normal "peak performance" sleep routine. Who could sleep, after all, with the lights and TV on?

That night, she went home turned off the lights and TV, closed the bedroom door, went to her side of the bed, turned on her "right" side and she slept like a baby.

Having a clear picture, including the sounds and feelings, of your peak performance state in any arena is so critical that the moment you create it, your performance will improve dramatically.

If your picture is not quite clear right now, don't worry about it. Keep asking yourself the five questions until it becomes crystal clear to you. If your picture is fuzzy, you may need to get more information about your outcome before you can make the picture in your mind clear.

MORE INFORMATION CLARIFIES THE PICTURE

A recent college graduate contacted me and told me that she had heard that I was doing something that sounded similar to what she wanted to do for a career. She told me she thought she wanted to do something called "corporate communications planning or consulting." She wasn't quite sure what was involved in the field, where to look for more information, or if she even had the right name for it. In other words, she had a fuzzy picture.

But she didn't let her fuzzy picture stop her. She was making calls to learn more about her area of interest so she could clarify her picture and then begin moving toward it. As it turned out, the field she needed to learn more about is called "organizational development" and I happened to know not only people in the field who she could talk to but also of a job opening in a related area. Simply by attempting to clarify her picture she had already begun to move closer to it.

Sometimes people are afraid to write down their goals because they fear that they might change their mind. That's perfectly all right. Peak Performers often change their goals as they get closer to them and identify pictures and goals that are even more compelling. If your goal changes, you'll simply get out a new piece of paper and write down your new goal. However, I strongly recommend that you *write down* your goals before you read on because, in the absence of goals, there is no peak performance.

STAYING IN THE HERE AND NOW

Once you have a clear picture in your mind, you need to shift your attention from your outcomes for the moment and focus on what you can do right now to get you there. The only place you can impact the future is in the present moment. Therefore, the most important thing you can do to achieve peak performance is to take action right now. Don't let your mind wander into the future to think about what will happen if you achieve your goal. Don't let your mind dwell on past successes or failures. Keep your mind focused only in the here and now, on the action you can take at this moment to move toward your goal. If you need practice to reach your goal, then practice right now. If you need additional resources or information to reach your goal, then make a list right now and start taking action to get those resources right now!

If you are in sales, stop thinking about the last call where you were thrown out. Stop thinking about that big sale you might get next week. If you need to talk to prospects to reach your goal, then get on the phone right now. Focus on this call, this customer, this customer's needs and this customer will turn into a big customer.

If you are a manager stop thinking about the person you'd like to hire or your superstar who left. Think instead about the staff you have and the projects on your desk right now. What can you do right now in the present moment to move yourself, your company and your career forward? Do that! After completing that task, repeat the process and ask yourself the same question again. Remember, the only place you can impact the future is in the present moment.

Probably the hardest pattern to adopt when trying to become a peak performer is the ability to stay in the here and now. The only way to affect the outcome is to focus on the present. The present is the only place you can impact the future. You've seen it happen any number of times in sports. A team celebrates too early. The players focus on the outcome, the win, instead of the process for getting there, only to have their competitors steal the win. The minute you look to the future or to the past, you are not in the present. The reason this can be so damaging to your results is if your mind is not in the present, your energy is not in the present.

My friend and mentor Chris Thorson says, "The energy goes where the mind goes." While you're doing a task, if you are thinking about anything except the task at hand, you are compromising your energy level. I've seen many sales people over the years calculating the commission they'll make on a piece of business, or fighting with others over the commission split, *before* they've confirmed the sale. Then, because they're focusing on the outcome instead of the process (meeting the customer's needs), they lose the sale.

The present moment is the only place you can impact the future. If you are completely focused on the process, you will see the results in the quality of your work. This is also what athletes call "the zone." They're not thinking about last week's competition or where they're going to display their medal if they win today's race.

When peak performers are asked what their strategy is for making it to the finals or for winning the gold medal, they repeatedly say they are concentrating on one competitor, one game or one win at a time. The true peak performers don't look beyond the present event. The minute they do, their energy goes where their mind goes and they won't win the present event because all of their energy isn't focused on it.

FOCUS ON THE PROCESS

The easiest way to stay in the here and now is to focus on the process. When I work with new sales people, I often give them a goal of 30–

40 cold calls a day because it keeps their minds focused on calling or seeing large numbers of customers, and they don't have time to dwell on the rejections.

Coaches often tell athletes to focus on their breathing. This keeps them in the here and now and keeps them from focusing on other competitors.

Focusing on your breathing is such a powerful method for staying in the present moment that it is used to achieve peak performances in most disciplines including yoga, dance, aerobics, weightlifting, archery, running, swimming, the martial arts, and singing. Many pregnant women take Lamaze classes to learn special breathing patterns for childbirth.

When I get frustrated or tense at the office, I often find that I'm holding my breath. By refocusing on my breathing, I can come back to the here and now and take the appropriate actions in the present moment to solve the problem that is creating my frustration.

If you've never had any instruction on proper breathing techniques, sign up for some yoga or martial arts classes or find a good singing or running coach. They all understand the finer points of breathing for peak performance.

Another way to keep your focus in the here and now is to key in on one small part of the process. Focus only on the ball or the computer keyboard or the customer's words.

I was a ski instructor for seven years yet sometimes I find I just don't ski as well as I'd like to ski. To help me focus on the process of skiing, my coach asked me to describe what it sounds like when I'm really skiing well. I've been skiing all of my life and I had never thought about what it sounded like. I could easily tell him what it looked like and how it felt, but I had no idea how it sounded.

The next day I was really "in the groove" on one run so I began to focus on what it sounded like. What I now find is that by skiing in a way that recreates that sound, I can ski "in the groove" all day!

DEALING WITH DISTRACTIONS

Distractions often keep us from focusing on the here and now. The most common distractions that kill a peak performance are change, risk, fear, surprises, stress, failure or even success.

Peak performers not only adapt to change, they embrace change. Peak performers understand that something has to change in order for them to reach their goal. After all, if nothing had to change, they would already be at the goal. Most people who are not peak performers see change as a threat or an obstacle. In fact, they often change only when forced.

Peak performers are always looking for a better way and an improved procedure. Peak performers are rarely content with the status quo.

Because peak performers are so open to change, they are also experts at handling surprises. They view surprises as gifts or opportunities to shine. They respond with the challenge response, saying to themselves, "Isn't this an interesting change? Now I'll get a chance to see how good I really am," or "Wow, I've never run a marathon in the snow before, I'll bet it'll help me to stay cool!"

Those who are not performing at their peak view surprises as wrenches in their plans or as evidence that they are victims of the universe. They wonder why they didn't see a surprise coming, or why they weren't warned. They try to blame others or fate or bad karma.

When a surprise occurs they are more likely to focus on the outcome and what may happen as a result of the surprise. As soon as they slip into any of these thought patterns, they are not focused on the present. The focused energy they need to deal successfully with the situation will also not be present.

My favorite example of this concept is from "Star Trek." Captain Kirk was in a training simulation and was given a no-win scenario to see how he would react under stress. He simply reprogrammed the simulator saying, "I don't believe in no-win scenarios."

This is an excellent insight into the belief system of a peak performer. (Yes, I know he's fictional, but the point remains the same.) By focusing on the action, he was able to remain in the here and now;

rather than being upset by the surprise, he was able to rise to the occasion and win even in a no-win scenario!

Peak performers also handle risk differently. The potential peak performer would rather fall short of his goals than take a risk. An athlete may not try out for the Olympics because he is afraid of failure. A sales person may not want to call on a potential new customer for fear that he may be rejected. What these people don't realize is that by not taking the risk they are *guaranteeing* failure. If they take action, they at least have the possibility of success.

What the peak performer realizes is that if he or she takes the risk and fails, the result is simply to have broken even. These performers either come away from the competition with a gold medal or with a lot more experience about what it will take to win next time. They can approach their actions with this mindset because they know how to eliminate or minimize the risk in their minds so that they can focus on the here and now and put their energy into producing the performance that is necessary to win.

Peak performers evaluate the worst thing that could happen to them if they attempt a performance. Then they ask themselves if they could handle the worst-case scenarios. If the answer is yes, then it's full speed ahead. If the answer is no, then they create options that will minimize the risk.

Several years ago I wanted to learn how to hang glide, but when I researched the sport further, I found that it didn't have the greatest safety record. Some of the most experienced pilots are in hang glider heaven. So I kept reading and asking questions and finally found a new invention. It's a parachute launcher that attaches to the top of the hang glider. If you lose control of the hang glider, you simply pull a trigger and float safely to the ground. With the risk minimized, I was ready to fly.

Peak performers also use another tool to help them minimize risks and anticipate surprises. They use a tool called scenario planning. You might also call it playing "What if…." They try to anticipate all the things that might go wrong and then develop a plan for how they would handle each of those scenarios.

The Shell Oil Company strategic planning team uses scenario planning to anticipate all of the possible shifts that might take place in the world's oil markets. In the early 1970s the company planned its possible reactions to a scenario that included the cutoff of Middle East oil. When OPEC imposed its oil embargo in 1973, Shell went into action. Because Shell's planners had thought, ahead of time, how they might handle such a situation, they were ready to move. They had a clear picture and were able to focus on the here and now. In a few short years they went from being the smallest of the world's major oil companies to number two.

Another distraction peak performers have mastered is failure. A focus on failure is a focus on outcomes. The moment you let failure take the wind out of your sails, you have left the here and now. The key is to treat failure as a learning experience, a stepping stone and a ladder to success. Find out what went wrong and what you will need to do differently next time. Then get moving on the next task that will help you to realize your goal.

Success can also be a distraction. Success is also an outcome. Too much focus on any outcome (even positive outcomes) takes you out of the here and now. Peak performers also treat success as a learning experience. When they win they analyze what went right and how they can use what they've learned in other areas of their lives. Interestingly, the peak performer views all outcomes, failures and successes, in the same light. All outcomes and all experiences are *feedback*.

NO MORE SECRETS, NO MORE WONDERING, NO MORE EXCUSES

What is the difference between the peak performer and the average person? The answer is no longer a mystery. Peak performers are able to draw a clear picture of what they want to accomplish. They are then able to put that picture aside and focus on the process that will get them there. They are able to overcome all distractions to stay in the here and now, the only place they know they can impact the future. So, now that *you* know the secrets, what is it that you want to accomplish?

7

TAKE AIM IN LIFE—WITH AMAZING ACCURACY

by Tony Alessandra, Ph.D., CSP, CPAE

Tony Alessandra is a former graduate professor of marketing. Since 1976 he has delivered nearly 2,000 presentations, authored 11 books, and been featured in more than 50 audio-video programs and films. He focuses on an integrated approach to marketing, sales and service, emphasizing how to outmarket, outsell and outservice the competition and how to sell value to turn targeted prospects into profitable, long-term customers. He currently owns a sales automation software company. Phone: 800-222-4383/619-459-4515; e-mail: DrTony A@alessanndra.com; web site: www.alessanndra.com.

Think about your favorite Olympic athlete, professional sports personality, or business super achiever. Do you think it's possible that he or she became successful without first setting up a target and then taking aim? Not likely. No matter what kind of archer you are, whether Olympic, professional, or recreational, without a target, your fulfillment is left to chance. That's not good enough.

Striving for and attaining goals makes life meaningful. People who have no goals feel emotionally, socially, spiritually, physically, and professionally unbalanced. This can only cause anxiety. People who have goals are respected by their peers; they are taken seriously. Making decisions that affect the direction of your life positively is a sign of strength. Goals create drive and positively affect your personality.

THE 3-PERCENT SOLUTION

Several years ago *Time* magazine reported the results of a national survey that found only 3 percent of those surveyed had written personal goals; 97 percent of the people had no goals at all or had only thought about them. They had not committed their goals to writing. Interestingly, the 3 percent who had written goals were found to have accomplished much more than any of the 97 percent.

STEPPING-STONES TO GREATNESS

Achievements come from awareness, which starts with evaluating your strengths and weaknesses in light of your current situation. You then expand your beliefs (assumptions) to accept more goals for yourself. This leads you to establish plans and expand your actions to eventually achieve your goals. The model for this process is:

AWARENESS > BELIEFS > GOALS > PLANS > ACTIONS >
ACHIEVEMENTS

One step leads to another. After an achievement, you reevaluate yourself and find that each new feather in your cap makes you feel capable of accomplishing more and more. Your beliefs (assumptions) then expand, making more goals possible. The effect gains momentum and snowballs. In this way, greatness is achieved by small stepping-stones.

RULES OF GOAL SETTING

Most people, when asked, "What are your goals in life?" say something like, "To be happy, healthy, and have plenty of money." On the surface these goals seem fine. However, if you think about goals in terms of leading to actions, they don't qualify. These types of goals don't have the key ingredients necessary to make them effective, workable goals. To begin organizing your goal setting, it is helpful to think about seven basic categories that can be delineated for goal-setting. These categories encompass the mental, physical, professional, financial, spiritual, family and social aspects of life.

Your goal must be personal. This means your goals must be uttered with sincerity. A goal must be something you *want* to do rather than something you think you *should* do. Know your reasons for having the goal. Whether you want to achieve a goal for status, money, or good health, or whatever reason—these reasons must be strong enough within you to fuel your desire to work to attain your goal.

Your goal must be positive. Take the following test: Don't think about green elephants! You can't do it; that's why an image of a green elephant immediately pops into your mind. It's an automatic response to think of the thing you're told not to think about. This is because the mind cannot refuse to think of something when instructed to do so. We tend to focus on ideas and actions from a positive framework. When you think a negative thought such as, "I will not smoke today," your mind automatically ends up thinking more about smoking than if you had phrased it differently. "I will breathe only clean air today" is a statement which serves the same purpose and is more effective.

Your goal must be written. Writing a goal down has effects which are a bit difficult to explain. It does, nonetheless, prove effective. Written goals take a jump in status from being nebulous thoughts (which you didn't care enough about to dignify as bona fide entities on paper). Perhaps their being written serves as a visual reminder and thus continually reconfirms their importance. Another possibility is that when things are "put in writing" they become official in our minds, reminiscent of the instructions accompanying the Ten

Commandments: "So let it be written, so let it be done." A written goal strengthens our commitment to accomplish it.

Your goal must be specific. If you set your goal by saying "I will increase my sales next year," chances are you won't do it. You need to be specific to avoid the lack of commitment which comes with being vague. A more workable and motivating goal would be, "I will increase my sales next year by 10 to 15 percent. This revised statement has several advantages. It defines the increase which you are striving for as well as the range of the desired increase. Giving yourself some leeway is more realistic than expecting to hit your goal at exactly 15 percent.

Your goal must be a challenge. A goal must motivate you to work harder than you have in the past. It must move you forward. Set your goals just beyond your reach so that you'll have to stretch a bit. The more you stretch, the more limber your goal achieving abilities will become.

Your goal must be realistic. Everything is relative to time and space. What is unrealistic today may be totally within reason five years from now. For years it was believed that the fastest a man could run a mile was in four minutes. It was unrealistic to aspire to running any faster until Dr. Roger Bannister broke the four-minute mile in 1954. Since then hundreds of runners have done the same. In any field, we never really know what the upper limits are. How, then, do we define realistic?

For our purposes, the best definition must come from you and your values. You must ask yourself, "What price am I willing to pay to accomplish this goal?" You should always weigh the payoffs and the sacrifices involved before coming to a conclusion. Whether or not a goal is realistic is ultimately your decision.

GOAL ACTION PLAN

Now that you know the rules for setting goals, you can apply them to the goals you set for yourself. What follows is a goal action plan that can be applied to each of the seven facets of your life. It would be a good idea to make your own action plans and use them for every goal you want to achieve. For each goal, your goal action plan must specify the following points:

Define your goal. Your first task is to determine whether your goal meets all six requirements of the rules listed above. If it does, then write it as clearly as possible at the top of the worksheet.

Examine obstacles that stand in your way. This is a time to guard against negative assumptions and other self-defeating thoughts. Remember the definition of realistic. An obstacle blocks you only if you let it. You should also write down your innovative ways of overcoming obstacles.

W.I.I.F.M. (What's in it for me?)Why do you want to achieve the goal? What kind of payoff is motivating you?

Plan your action. You need to carefully list the steps you will take which will bring you closer to your goal. The smaller the increments, the easier they will be to accomplish. There is a German proverb which says, "He who begins too much accomplishes little."

Project a target date for your goal. State your deadline range, such as, "between March 15 and April 1." Think carefully about the amount of time you need. Too little time will increase the pressure and frustrate you. Too much time may reduce your drive.

Know how you'll measure your success. Goals should be described in terms of the final outcome of an activity rather than as the activity. This is part of being specific. Instead of saying, "I will be running more in four to six months," you could say "I'll be running three miles instead of two miles in four to six months."

Feel free to alter the worksheet to suit your needs. The important thing is to fill it out completely and to keep it visible for each of your key goals in each of the seven facets of your life. Put them in a place where you will see them every day. Check off items as you complete them. Use them to chart your progress and take pride in your accomplishments.

Visualizing: what you see is what you get

Visualization is an indispensable tool in helping people attain their goals. Olympic athletes have proven that visualization is an effective substitute for real practice. In visualizing your goals, you will live your accomplishments in your mind's eye. The more of the five senses you can involve in this exercise, the greater your chances are of accomplishment.

Let's say, for example, that you want to be the Salesperson of the Year in your company. You know that each year an awards banquet is given during which a plaque is presented to the year's sales leader. You may choose to focus on this banquet for your visualization exercise. Here's what you do:

Make yourself comfortable, close your eyes, and relax. Slowly and systematically use each of the five senses to imagine what you would be experiencing at the banquet.

Sight. Imagine what you would see there. You'd see other salespeople and their spouses. Imagine what they are wearing. You'd see tables decorated and waiters scurrying about. You'd see the bar and people standing around talking. Maintain the image for several minutes.

Sound. What would you hear? You'd hear the chatter of people. You would hear laughter, the tinkling of glasses, music from a band, people talking. You would also continually hear people coming up to congratulate you. Imagine that.

Smell. Imagine all the smells you'd experience. Women's perfume, food, alcohol, men's cologne, the smell of polyester suits (not yours, of course).

Feel. What would your tactile sensations be? You'd feel people brushing against you in the crowded room. You'd feel others shaking your hand.

Taste. Taste in your mind the champagne you'll be drinking. Taste the food you'll be eating. Experience the sweet taste of success—in advance!

Most importantly, imagine the exhilaration you'll feel when your name is called to receive the award. Take your time during this exercise and enjoy it. The more you can "visually" attend this banquet, the more motivated you will become. (You might even learn something about the catering business!)

THE VISUALIZATION FILE

To aid in your visualization exercise, you might want to start a visualization file. This is an envelope or file into which you put pictures, clippings, letters, and other reminders of what it will be like to succeed. Your file should also contain letters or awards which you have received in the past. Anything that makes you feel good about yourself can be included in the file. It can then be used as a source of motivation and inspiration, especially if you begin to feel a little down or unmotivated. We all need to be reminded of our past accomplishments once in a while. Be your own best friend and remind yourself!

ROLE MODELS

Many people concentrate only on the goal they wish to attain.

There's more to the picture: Successful people in every field have certain character traits in common. These common traits do not occur by chance, they are an integral part of goal attainment. It is worth your time to analyze the constructive characteristics of people who are now where you'd like to be.

One effective method to study character traits is to choose role models. These are people to look up to and emulate. Your choices can include people who are dead or living, as long as you are familiar with their personalities and accomplishments.

Harry Truman knew the value of role models. When he was in the White House he reportedly went into the Lincoln bedroom, looked at the late president's picture and asked "What would Lincoln have done if he were in my situation?" The answers to this question often gave Truman the insight and direction he was seeking. This process worked because Truman felt Lincoln was a man worth emulating.

In choosing a role model, several things must be kept in mind. Keep your role model off the pedestal. There is no doubt that you will choose people whom you see as being "above" you because of what they have accomplished. That's good. What isn't good is to put them on a pedestal, thereby making them larger than life. We are all human. We all have strengths and weaknesses. You must not lose this perspective on people. Putting role models on pedestals only further separates you from them.

Isolate their strong points. You need to look at the person you wish to emulate and analyze the precise qualities he or she possesses which you need to acquire. Sit down and write out the characteristics which seem to encourage his or her success.

Use concrete examples of behaviors which you can adapt to our own situation. For example, if you admire a corporate executive, one of the many traits you might isolate is her policy of "early to bed, early to rise." Write out approximately when she does each and why. You can then do the same and know the reason why you're doing it. Remain yourself. Quite often the tendency when admiring someone is to try to become his clone. People who seem to "have it all together" have done all the "work" for you. All you have to do is imitate them. This is a dangerous way to think because you are not working on your own personality.

In the final analysis, you are you. It is impossible to become exactly like someone else. And why should you want to? So remain yourself while you acquire new traits to help you achieve your goals.

Sometimes it is helpful to have a symbol of another person's virtues. This symbol will actually remind you of that person and his or her qualities. It can take the form of a picture, a possession (e.g., your father's pocket watch), or some abstract thing such as a rock. It will be useful as long as it makes the association in your mind.

MENTORS

A mentor is someone you admire under whom you can study. Throughout history the mentor–protégé relationship has proven quite fruitful. Socrates was one of the early mentors. Plato and Aristotle studied under him and later emerged as great philosophers in their own rights. Mentors are worth cultivating if you can find one.

The same cautions hold true here as for any role model. It is better to adapt their philosophies to your life than to adopt them. Be suspicious of any mentor who seeks to make you dependent on him. It's better to have him teach you how to fish than to have him catch the fish for you. That way you'll never starve.

Under the right circumstances mentors make excellent role models. The one-to-one setting is highly conducive to learning as well as to friendship.

THE THOUGHT DIET

The Thought Diet, developed by my friend and colleague Jim Cathcart, is a tool that you can use on a daily basis to help you become the person who will achieve your goals. On the thought diet card, you break down your goals into daily actions that are bite-sized and easy to do. By identifying the steps along the way, the thought diet will keep you from being overwhelmed by your lofty goals.

RULES OF THE THOUGHT DIET

1. Read the thought diet card every day. It is best to read it *both* in the morning when you rise and in the evening before you retire. Repetition is an integral part of learning and will help you stay on target.
2. Avoid associating with people who drag you down emotionally. Associate with people who are positive and from whom your optimism can grow.
3. Make your adherence to the thought diet meaningful. Read and fill out the card sincerely. Don't just go through the motions.

PRIMARY GOAL

The second section of the card, after the rules, is a space where you write that goal which is strongest and affects your motivation the most at this point in time.

DAILY GROWTH

The third section of the card deals with traits you are developing. Write out five key traits that you need to develop to achieve your goal. State these personal qualities in ways which adhere to the rules of goal setting.

ACTION PLAN

The fourth section of the card is the action section. Here you will write out the "minimum daily standards" which you will perform every day to move you closer to your goal. Be specific.

The following are some examples of minimum daily standards:

Mental: I will spend 15 minutes every evening doing visualization exercises.

Physical: I will do at least five push-ups and ten sit-ups every morning.

Professional: I will read something related to my career for at least 15 minutes before going to bed.

Financial: I will keep a complete record of every expense and financial transaction.

Spiritual: Each day I will do one good deed to help someone less fortunate than I.

Family: I will relax over dinner and enjoy a meaningful uninterrupted conversation with my family.

Social: I will take time during my coffee breaks in the office to chat with coworkers.

INSPIRATION AND MOTIVATION

Read the thought diet card twice a day until everything becomes a habit. Once you've developed constructive habits, you can move on to new goals and behaviors. Fill out a new card and practice the new challenges every day until they become habits. In this way, you will painlessly move closer and closer to your goals.

The dividends reaped by investing in yourself are unlike any other found in the financial world. When you clarify your values and set goals in all the major areas of your life—mental, physical, family, social, spiritual, professional, and financial—the target appears in front of you at very close range. Choices become infinitely easier to make because you are aiming at something specific, and you've taken a giant step toward hitting your goals…with amazing accuracy.

8

WIN THE GOLD WITH METTLE

by George Walther, CSP, CPAE

George Walther is a professional speaker, author and acknowledged expert in communication effectiveness. His *Phone Power* book, seminars, and audio-video tapes are regarded as definitive guides. In *Power Talking,* he shows how to become more positive, persuasive and popular in conversation. His latest title, *Upside-Down Marketing,* focuses on a new approach to maximizing profit leverage opportunities. His books appear in many foreign language editions. Phone: 425-255-2900; e-mail: GeoWalther@aol.com.

I don't even like sports. I ignore the World Series and have never wagered on a Super Bowl. The last basketball game I played was in high school. Yet, I always look forward to watching the Olympics and I especially enjoy the televised profiles of the Olympic athletes. Their personal stories always fascinate me. Each athlete seems to have struggled with some major hardship leading up to the competition: health challenges, family tragedies, financial difficulties or some other obstacle to excellence. Each Olympian has triumphed over significant setbacks.

What's the one experience that Olympic athletes encounter more than any other? Defeat! Those at the top get there by enduring years—even decades—of grueling, torturous training, only to lose most of their competitive events. Yet, many—far more than will ever win any medals—are still Olympians in terms of the quality of their performances.

If medals were necessary to identify true Olympians, there wouldn't be many of them. A very small percentage of the athletes who strive to compete, or even of those who actually make it to the games, ever win a medal. The true measure of an Olympic performer depends much more on his *mettle* than on his medals.

The dictionary defines *mettle* as a "quality of temperament or disposition; vigor and strength of spirit or temperament; staying quality." For synonyms, try "courage" and "stamina." Isn't that what Olympic performance in life really means? If Dan Jansen had never won his gold medal, wouldn't you still think of him as an Olympic-class performer? It's when they encounter defeat, daunting circumstances, and unforeseen setbacks that Olympians show their mettle. Few Olympians actually win medals, but true Olympians always demonstrate their mettle.

SHOW YOUR METTLE

The same simple and systematic actions that can get you the gold in sports, can also serve you when pursuing outstanding performances in any endeavor. Whether in athletics, parenting, business, academic achievement, career growth, or any other pursuit, it's your ability to persevere in the face of daunting challenges that makes for Olympic performances. And even if you don't participate in or care about sports you can strive to perform as an Olympian in most other areas of your life.

People who achieve extraordinary levels of accomplishment in any field, whether it's raising a healthy family, making significant career advances, or shaving tenths of a second off a world-record time in an Olympic event, also encounter and overcome the most significant setbacks. In fact, those very setbacks help mold them into Olympic-level performers.

I'm convinced that the key to upgrading your performance levels—in any undertaking—is to concentrate on triumphing in setback situations and converting them into mettle-molding opportunities.

HANDLE ONE SETBACK AT A TIME

Setbacks will inevitably present themselves. There's no need to feel overwhelmed about the grandiose task of creating a lifetime of Olympic performances; just concentrate on how you handle the very next setback that comes along.

By concentrating on one setback at a time and developing your own strategy for dealing with the next one, you create a track record for reaping value from those situations that may appear to others as disasters.

When "bad" things happen, two distinct groups of people exhibit very different responses. Most people shut down, become morose and depressed, and whine and moan. They view and interpret the event as a major obstacle preventing progress in their lives. Others, the true Olympians, immediately kick into gear and get busy taking action. Winners don't whine.

You can employ Olympian setback strategies in dealing with your own impediments, whether they're athletic, academic, or accounting; whether they're related to profiting, parenting, or partnering.

Think of the six following traits as Olympian skill sets that you can learn when you encounter setbacks.

DECIDE TO MANAGE THE SITUATION

Command and control are the keys to triumphing in tough times. Taking command of the situation means managing it and actively seeking to extract value in the form of lessons. Perhaps concentrated physical action is appropriate in your situation. You may need to get busy networking with colleagues, or talking to customers, or scheduling a "family meeting," or updating your old résumé. Don't assume that command requires physical action. Sometimes a lack of action is exactly what's needed.

The greatest personal challenge I've encountered in my lifetime presented me with a wonderful opportunity to grow and develop my own setback strategies. On almost the same day, both my marriage and my father were pronounced dead. Of course, the official, legal termination of my marriage came after long and agonizing legal proceedings and a good deal of struggling. When the trial was over and the judge dismissed us, I felt tremendous relief and believed that I'd finally be able to unwind emotionally for a while. I didn't count on getting a disturbing phone call the very next morning and learning of my father's rapidly deteriorating health. I came to view my father's sudden death as an unexpected test of how much I could handle.

In my situation, I decided that one of the best ways for me to take command of the setback was to be still and listen to my heart and soul. I've always been a very active, take-charge "doer," so backing off wasn't easy for me. When I held back and stopped trying to "handle" everything by undertaking some action, I was much better off and much more effective. I found that my best course of command was to do what seemed like doing nothing.

FOCUS ON CLEAR GOALS

Actually, what I did was a far cry from "nothing." I quietly and seriously established a series of specific, prioritized goals, wrote them out, and kept a copy in plain sight as a reminder of where I needed to focus my energy. The very first, most important goal was to stay sane! In order to do so, I knew I needed to invest time in relaxation and introspection, letting my heart and mind go to work without my active, conscious involvement.

Goal setting is the discipline that's so often cited as the one that sets winners apart from losers. There's a lot more to using goals effectively than simply deciding what you want, though that's certainly a critical step. For an Olympic athlete, one goal may be to place as a medalist in some preliminary competition. For a business person, it may be to win a critical piece of new business. Or, your personal goal may be to get some derailed personal relationship back on course.

Early in my business career, I worked as an advertising executive at a major international advertising agency where I helped develop advertising plans for major clients including Continental Airlines, Van de Kamps foods, and McCulloch Chain Saws. During the training phase of my work at the agency, I was taught to fill in "Key Data Sheets." These were single page forms which were used to set the direction for any given advertisement or commercial.

The Key Data Sheet included blank spaces for specific details like ad sizes and publications, target audience demographics, legal disclaimers, etc. But the most important part of the form was the first, and it was also the hardest for me to grasp. There, at the very top of the page, were two blank sections to be completed before filling in anything else: "Objective" and "Strategy."

It took me a long time to understand the distinction between those concepts, but once I finally grasped the importance of setting clear objectives and backing them up with sound strategies, I found I could use the same technique in many areas of my life. Now, years later, I still use the Objective/Strategy exercise as the basis for all kinds of goal setting in life, particularly when I'm handling setback situations. Where do I want to go? What do I seek to accomplish? What is my aim? What is my goal, or objective?

The *strategy* part is the road map that guides me toward my goal. With a strategy, I become accountable for whether or not I'm actually doing what's necessary to triumph over the setback. For the athlete, it may be a specific training regimen, or a set of performance milestones leading toward the eventual performance goal.

In business, the strategies are the specific plans that lead you to the attainment of your objectives and may involve drawing on outside resources, blocking time to tackle critical activities, or re-allocating financial and manpower resources.

In my very personal example of coping with my biggest setbacks, I set seemingly simple goals or objectives, and backed each one with a set of strategies. In order of priority, I determined to:

1. Stay sane;

2. Be the best parent I could be; and,

3. Do a superb job on the platform each time I delivered a speech;

4. *And that's all!*

While coping with my own divorce and my father's death, I knew that I'd be doing well to achieve my first three goals. Seeking new clients, taping a new training video series, and establishing a post-divorce financial plan were all important goals, and they were also beyond what I knew I could realistically accomplish at the time. I decided not to strategize how I might achieve them. My fourth goal was to keep my energies focused on achieving the first three, and not get distracted by attempting to do too much.

Simple, clear, reasonable goals work best. Likewise, clear, direct strategies linked to each goal are necessary to make them come true. In my case, the strategies were as simple as the goals:

Stay sane by taking ample time off, treating myself well with daily physical exercise, seeking out supportive friends to help me talk through troubling situations, following a spiritual path, and looking for opportunities to laugh and see beauty.

Be a great parent by putting my daughter at the very top of my priorities, maximizing the time that she has my full attention, getting involved in father-daughter activities like the excellent YMCA Indian Princess program, and giving her loving relief from the inevitable stress any child experiences in a divorce.

Do a great job on the platform by limiting my expectations to achieving just these three priority goals, to ensure that I don't turn up at speaking engagements unprepared and exhausted. By not overextending myself, I could perform well on the platform.

SEARCH FOR LESSONS

Setbacks, while inconvenient, are ripe with unmatched growth opportunities, if you look for the lessons. Olympians encounter setbacks on their paths and say, "What can I learn from that, and how will I perform differently based on what I just learned?"

It seems that we all want to understand *why* things happen. Unfortunately, some of the answers we seek are tough, elusive, and seemingly incomprehensible ones. "Why did my child die in a car crash?" "Why did the airline lose my luggage just when I needed it most?" "Why did I get sick before the critical meeting I needed to attend?" In my view, the events just *are*. and the only answer to "why?" is, "Because this setback gives me a perfect opportunity to learn some new lessons otherwise unavailable to me."

Consciously manage your language

How you verbally describe a setback reveals and shapes the way you think about and learn from them. A typical "loser script" goes like this: "Why did this have to happen? Just when my career was really rolling along, my company was acquired and now I've been notified that I'm likely to be laid off. I'll never get another job this good."

The "winner" Olympian, on the other hand, says, "This has happened. My company has been acquired. Now, I have the opportunity to either prove myself so valuable that the new organization can't do without me, or search out an opportunity to build on the tremendous career advances I've made in the last couple of years."

In *Power Talking: 50 Ways to Say What You Mean and Get What You Want,* I examine how you can foster the mindset that interprets setbacks as positive opportunities. This is a skill you can develop, one word and phrase at a time.

A good starting point is to purge the words "I failed..." from your vocabulary. Whenever you're tempted to describe an event in this way, substitute, "I learned..." to help your mind focus on the lessons to be gleaned.

Similarly, you'll help maintain a positive attitude by substituting "challenge" or "opportunity" when most people would be saying "problem." If you say "We're going to have a *problem* notifying our customers about this product recall," you conjure up all kinds of negative experiences you naturally want to avoid. Who likes problems?

On the other hand, making a simple word replacement and saying, "We're going to have a *challenge* notifying our customers about this product recall," completely changes the sense of what you're saying. Olympians rise to challenges. The subliminal effect of changing a few words can help spur your mind to conceive creative solutions to the challenging situation, rather than dreading and fleeing from the problems.

WELCOME SPIRITUAL ASSISTANCE

Praying never used to make sense to me. I still have trouble even saying the word. I'd watch those Olympic athletes on TV and note that they often bowed their heads and prayed silently before their events. I'd say to myself, "Who do they think they're kidding? Surely they don't really believe that some God is watching the competition, pulling for one praying competitor, helping him along because he prayed?" I figured it was just for display, so that the worldwide viewing audience would think the athlete was pious or religious. Anyway, how could it possibly help?

Then, at age 45, I finally understood what they were doing and why. I prayed for the very first time. As a child, I had knelt by my bed, mimicking what I saw kids doing on family TV shows. I thought of it as a dramatic performance.

My first real prayer was for peace in my adult family. During my very emotional divorce proceedings, an intense outburst from my wife left me shaken and shaking. I was living at Alki Beach in Seattle, so after she drove away, I walked out from my apartment, my heart racing, and sat on a big driftwood log that had washed up on the pebbly shore. I just sat quietly, not knowing what to do. After half an hour of blankly staring out at the passing ferry boats plying Puget Sound, I heard someone talking.

It was me. I was talking, but nobody else was around to hear me. I listened to myself saying, "I want peace. I don't know what to do. I need help. This situation has mushroomed beyond my ability to apply any rational strategy to fix it."

I realized I was praying. I still feel more comfortable calling it "meditating" or "seeking spiritual guidance." Regardless of its label, for the first time in my life, I was calling on some spiritual power to help me during a severe setback. I didn't direct my message to any particular entity; I wasn't talking specifically to Buddha or Vishnu or Jesus Christ. I was praying *for* an outcome, rather than *to* some entity.

Olympic athletes are probably not asking God to give them a little shove so they'll finish ahead of the others. Olympians pray for the strength, ability, and courage to do their very best, to outperform themselves. That's just what I was doing at Alki Beach.

I've come to discover that prayer is effective and that praying for a positive outcome helps, whether you're pursuing athletic goals, handling touchy parenting issues, orchestrating business negotiations, or navigating divorce difficulties. As I see it, prayer is not a request for outside intervention so much as a calling on my own personal inner strength. It seems that people access only a small fraction of their abilities, physical and mental. Praying is simply becoming still and calling on God and your inner well of strength to make available more helping resources.

One thing prayer or meditation provides for me is calmness. When I feel uptight, as an athlete must before a major contest, the act of praying or meditating helps me to focus on the outcome I seek, and quiets the distractions which could clutter my mind and interfere with my finest functioning, especially when I face setbacks.

KICK INTO ACTION QUICKLY AT THE FIRST SIGN OF SETBACK

Soon after reading this page, you'll experience some setback. I hope it will be something small, just a minor inconvenience. How you react in the first critical moments will set the tone for your handling of this incident, the next inevitable setback, and by extension, the rest of your life! It's the setbacks in life, and how we react to them, that always provide the best opportunities for developing Olympic performance skills. Look forward to setbacks, they're your opportunities to turn in an Olympic performance. As a culture, we North Americans seem obsessed with beating others, rather than outperforming ourselves. We pursue gold medals, and focus the spotlights on those very few who triumph over their competitors, but we overlook those who simply perform superbly. What truly counts in life is your mettle, not your medals.

9

WINNING THE GOLD MEDAL
FOR COMMUNICATIONS

by Francis X. Maguire

An acknowledged authority on quality, productivity and communications, Frank Maguire shares his experience from a career that has taken him from the highest levels of America's most respected businesses to auditoriums full of eager listeners. As the first senior vice president of industrial relations at Federal Express, he created the corporate culture which led to Fortune Magazine naming the company "The Top Corporation of the Decade" and recipient of the 1991 Malcolm Baldrige National Quality Award. Frank Maguire's impressive history also includes assignments as director of program development at ABC, senior vice president at Kentucky Fried Chicken and director of market and public relations program for American Airlines. Phone: 888-437-2656; e-mail: HearthFXM@aol.com.

Undoubtedly, the original Adam and intellectuals from Benjamin Franklin to Adam Smith to Peter Drucker and John Naisbitt would concur that today's pace of change is occurring at much faster rates than ever before. In fact, according to futurist Faith Popcorn, while 1940 to 1990 represented 50 years of change, 1990 to 2000 (only 10 years) will represent another 50 years of change, and from 2000 to 2005 (just five years) we'll actually experience another 50 years of change. In short, that means that in 15 short years, from the year 1990 to 2005, we will have actually experienced 100 years of change! Every day we witness a unique period of transition and shake-out for American business. Acquisitions, mergers, bankruptcies, start-ups, shut-downs and new strategic alliances occur on a daily basis. The hard, cold fact is that those business executives who are ready to embrace change but have not planned for it, won't make it. On the other hand, those who embrace change, and do plan for it, may succeed. Frankly, there are no guarantees.

What is even more interesting is that we are also experiencing a fundamental shift in what constitutes power in business (or in life, for that matter). No longer does the corporation or the person with muscle or money rule. The power now lies with those who know how to continuously adapt to new technologies and can access, analyze and communicate information quickly and concisely. Size and money still play a role, but today it is those firms or executives who know how to use the resources of the information age to supply innovative, appropriate and timely solutions to their customers' problems that will survive and thrive.

WINDOW OF OPPORTUNITY

Thus, there is unquestionably a unique window of opportunity right now for America's corporations and executives to go for the gold.

Many of the winning elements are already in place: technology that provides full and immediate information, willing workers, experienced management, a proud history and loyal (although increasingly demanding) customers.

A lot has been accomplished by American management towards adapting to today's rapid changes; however, the magnitude of what remains to be accomplished is also impressive. But, it is doable.

However, whether or not adaptation is accomplished depends entirely on an openness and willingness on the part of American management to change. And a major part of that change involves effective communication.

EMPLOYEE MORALE CRISIS

Corporate America has a major communications problem which has created a crisis in terms of employee morale. The work force is confused. They're confused because they are confronted with change on a daily basis when they would much rather avoid change. We all know that it's human nature to resist change. This problem is then compounded by the latest technology which brings us change "live," as it happens, all around the world.

What's even more threatening to people, however, is change coupled with ambiguity. People are very threatened when they feel that they are not getting the full story of what is happening within their own company. This stressful combination really hits home to employees, directly affecting their lives in many ways. After all, there is nothing more disturbing to people than the unknown. The pain of uncertainty is worse than the certainty of pain.

Nowadays, American workers are seeing constantly changing management teams. Senior management is perceived as remote and indifferent. Employees hear words like re-engineering, consolidation, cost containment and downsizing, while they're being asked to work harder, smarter and longer hours. They're receiving a wide variety of conflicting messages. And, in the absence of solid information, they are open to all kinds of misinformation, rumors, undigested data and speculation about their company, its future, and as a result, their own futures.

These perceptions become their reality, adding up to a significant and pervasive problem. A problem which, more than any other factor, smothers the kind of enthusiasm and winning attitudes which are part of any successful enterprise. Morale and confidence in the company plunge to the lowest levels and each team member begins heading toward his or her own goal instead of one single goal.

COMMUNICATION CURE

These problems are systemic in any organization, in any team effort. And they all stem from poor communication—and can be solved with effective communication. Cumulatively, unmotivated, "invalidated" employees can sap the productive energy of a company. However, if the communication problems are dealt with and resolved, those same players can release a surge of positive energy and imagination which can transform an ordinary work place into a hub of participatory excellence and quality. As one of our country's greatest generals, Dwight D. Eisenhower, put it: "The most important ingredient in winning wars is morale." Yes, morale can make or break a team.

Indeed, the rising tide lifts all boats. Effective communication is a multiplying force within a company that can raise morale so that everyone benefits. Winning athletic teams have always known the importance of effective communication in raising morale to reach goals. Vince Lombardi, former coach of the Green Bay Packers, knew the importance of high morale: "The spirit, the will to win, and the will to excel are the things that endure. These qualities are so much more important than the events that occur." College football coach Lou Holtz also recognized the importance of morale and the effect communication has on morale as he turned several losing teams, including the University of Notre Dame, into winning teams during his career. By stressing the effective communication of goals and a vision, he built understanding and togetherness, and then utilized the diverse talents of each team member.

A TEAM-WIDE CULTURE SHARES A VISION

At the core of high morale is the need for a team-wide culture which incorporates a shared vision, shared knowledge, and shared responsibility. Again, let's consider Lou Holtz. Here's a man who as a 12-year-old child already knew his vision. (Visions are important for individual goals as well as for team goals.) While many didn't believe in him, his pursuit of his vision to become Notre Dame's head football coach never left him. And despite what many people perceived as handicaps, he chose to persistently pursue his goal....and his dream became a reality! That same determination holds true for many Olympic heroes—from track star Wilma Rudolph to ice skating great Scott Hamilton—both of whom overcame terrific odds to achieve their visions. Major league manager Tommy Lasorda was absolutely correct when he said, "The difference between the impossible and the possible lies in a man's determination." And determination is only possible with a vision.

Someone once asked Helen Keller how she could bear the pain of not being able to see, to which she replied, "Being without sight is not the worst thing that can happen to a person. The people I feel sorry for are those who have no vision." Without vision there is no desire, no commitment, no determination. Vision is the starting point of every creation. And as NFL coach Tom Flores said, "A total commitment is paramount to reaching the ultimate in performance."

A LACK OF VISION IS EASY TO SPOT

If a positive corporate attitude is sometimes hard to identify and define, there is little problem in sensing its absence in an individual or a group. A losing team mentality is devastating. It turns active and creative human energy into cynicism and hostility—into resistance. It puts an end to pride, to achievement, to initiative. It isolates people from each other and develops the "us against them" mentality at all levels of the team.

America's corporations have a world-class team of players whose productivity can be exponentially enhanced through the leadership of a unified management team which is responsive to the needs of the customer and which communicates clear, consistent and compelling messages about the directions and workings of the company. In short, it is the team which shares a vision, shares the knowledge necessary to aim for the right targets, and shares the determination and responsibility for achieving the vision that will win the gold. That's Lou Holtz' working principle. Interestingly, this concept of making every team member "an owner of the dream" is also the basic premise of total quality management.

The era of the quick fix and the off-the-shelf remedy is mercifully over. Instead, a solid manager-based system of employee communications can direct the vision and energy of a company to the customer-contact managers and staff who should have the knowledge and authority needed to quickly make confident and informed decisions in the marketplace. Today's business gurus call it "empowerment." In essence, empowerment is simply "common-sense decision-making." Employees are empowered when they have the ability to make decisions based on a solid understanding of a common vision or goal.

MANAGERS ARE THE CONDUIT

Managers are key. The manager is the mediator, teacher, motivator and model—a coach who knows the realities of the local, increasingly diverse work force as well as the vision of the company. There will be little productivity, improvisation, initiative or enthusiasm unless there is a manager who embodies this understanding for his players. Communication is the process. The manager is the agent.

WE COMMUNICATE, INTENTIONALLY OR NOT

Communication will be the test of the twenty-first century. We are the communicating species. As individuals and as groups (even sports teams), we employ an elaborate system of symbols and signals to create an environment of ideas, emotions and attitudes. We cannot *not* communicate. We are always sending out messages—not always well, but always. We communicate by our presence, by our choices, by our words, by the complex nuances or our silent language.

Fundamentally, human communication is an interactive process in which a message is sent, received, filtered and responded to. To fully understand ourselves and our organization it is critical that we understand each of these steps in this complex human activity carefully.

A corporation is a communicating entity with many audiences: the public, customers, competitors, government, stockholder, suppliers and employees. The perceptions of these groups are critical to the company's ability to operate and to thrive in a complex and increasingly competitive environment. Communication directly affects these perceptions, which means productivity and profitability are directly dependent on effective communication. Frankly, no company can be much better than the quality of its communication.

So, indeed, communication will be the test of the modern corporations—especially in today's information age. The information age is characterized by the democratization of information and a decentralization of decision making. They go together. Technology has increased the speed and amount of information incredibly. In fact, in a Rockhurst College publication, author Patricia Wilson claims that "one issue of the *New York Times* now contains more information than a Renaissance man would have read in his entire lifetime." P. S. Wurman, in *Information Anxiety*, says that the amount of available information now doubles every five years. It's information overload.

RESOURCES FOR QUALITY COMMUNICATION

But information does not equal thinking. Top information overload with customer expectations that require on-the-spot decisions and the potential for stressed employees is incredible. Like the soccer player in the middle of a tough game, an employee must be able to think on his feet. Therefore, today's employees need information which is candid, timely and thorough so that they can think effectively and quickly and become "professional knowledge workers."

To succeed in today's society of communications, the key resources are information, knowledge and creativity. And there is only one place to find these resources—within our people. The good coaches know this fact. Today's innovative corporations know it as well. Yet, you can't just hire people and expect to tap those key resources immediately. Today's atmosphere requires that people possess and use the key skills of thinking, learning and creativity, and that those skills continually be refined and encouraged.

THINKING SKILL

Thinking is the ability to synthesize and make generalizations, to categorize, to draw inferences, to distinguish fact from opinion, to use facts to analyze a problem. Information is no substitute for thinking.

In fact, the more information we have, the greater the need for competent thinking. It's the quandary of the information age: there is an abundance of data, but what good is that information if no one can sort it all out? Thinking is now as basic as reading.

LEARNING SKILL

In a world that is constantly changing, the ability to learn is essential. There is no one subject or set of subjects that will make an individual or a team successful in the short term, much less the long term. Thus, the most important skill to acquire and encourage now is learning how to learn. Yet that requires humility. "You have to be able to concede...that there are those who are better and more clever than yourself," wrote author Doris Lessing in an article entitled, "Learning How to Learn." Everyone, including managers, must admit that it simply is impossible to know everything about everything.

CREATIVITY SKILL

Creativity is one area where few business people feel competent or comfortable. Most people think creativity is for the scientist, the author, or the musical genius, not for the typical manager. But in this new information-rich, decentralized, global society, creativity has become valued in business and can be a corporation's competitive edge. Emphasizing creativity means unleashing the special talents of people to discover the right market niche or that final bug in the new computer system. It can be found in the salesperson who writes the proposal that penetrates the Chinese market. Or, creativity can be fostered in a manger to redesign an organization chart into a decentralized, customer-focused network. Creativity can be found or developed in anyone with an open mind who wants to meet the challenges that change brings.

These key skills—thinking, learning and creativity—are necessary to achieve visions and require change for everyone, from leaders and managers to team members. But, these skills will not be practiced unless their importance is consistently communicated and reinforced. Unfortunately, experience has confirmed that many corporations look upon communication as a kind of cosmetic overlay on the serious business of the company or as a bag of techniques designed to keep the public and the employees at peace. However, the communication dimension must be an integral part of the business of the corporation, because it can be the quickest and most cost-effective way of advancing the company's vision.

After all, there are no systems which are people proof. And getting the most out of your people is the cleanest and most direct path to progress and greater profitability. But, only if they share a vision, share the knowledge and share the responsibility.

MANAGERS AS MESSENGERS

If people are the brain of the corporation, then effective, honest communication is the central nervous system, and the manager is the soul, the source of information and motivation. Think about it—if managers are credible, the company is credible. The manager is the key factor in the triad of management, employees and customers.

The manager becomes the messenger and the message. And what that manager communicates is crucial because great work places are defined not so much by wages and working conditions as by feelings, attitudes and relationships.

Just look at the situation through the eyes of the employees. People don't show up in the morning with the idea of doing a mediocre job.

They want to make a difference, to contribute to the enterprise, to feel good about themselves and the job they're doing. In a time of disintegrating institutions, they want to belong to a group that does meaningful work and does it well. And people need to know that they have contributed in a positive manner. Keep in mind that the world constantly asks them, "What's your name and what do you do?" Both answers are important to people, to their pride.

FOUR I's

There are four qualities that managers need to practice themselves and cultivate in their team members. These can be summed up in a simple "Four I's" rubric: Informed, Involved, Inner-directed and In touch.

Informed. To be informed is to know the essence of something...knowing what something is all about without knowing all about something. It's knowing how to learn. In an age of information overload, it means knowing how to control information and data. If employees have this sense of how the system works and where things fit in the larger picture, they will be better able to deal with the particulars of their job. Professionals require this sense of wholeness.

Involved. To be involved is to have a personal stake in something—to be interested, absorbed and concerned. It means to feel that you make a difference. It is the opposite of putting in a day's work, getting by. It's the determination that winning coaches instill in their team members.

Inner-directed. If people are informed and involved, the motivation for quality performance will come from inside them, from a sense of self-esteem and self-confidence which will release their creative and positive energies. The impetus to achieve will be a response to the worthwhileness of the task and not merely from the external sanctions of authority, reward and punishment. The principal satisfaction of such a worker comes from the inside out.

John McKay, NFL coach, says it succinctly: "I am a big believer in the 'mirror test.' All that matters is if you can look in the mirror and honestly tell the person you see there that you've done your best."

In touch. "Reach out," says the commercial for one phone company.

Today that is a mandate for marketers in this era of enlightened and informed consumers. It means knowing, respecting and feeling customer concerns. It means knowing how to translate industry jargon into clear, intelligible language. It means building a bridge between the way business talks and the way customers talk. It means providing accurate, useful information with flexibility and with humility. Again, being in touch with your customer—and your employee, who is an internal customer, for that matter—is crucial to success today.

Once again, the manager is the soul of the team. The manager is the person who personalizes the "professional knowledge worker" strategy, who injects passion and feeling into the task. And, although sports metaphors have often been overused, it is helpful to look upon today's manager not as a boss but as a coach. The manager is the teacher, the motivator, the trainer, the model. The manager stands up for the players. The manager sets the tone. The manager monitors the execution of the plan in an informed and improvisional fashion.

And, in all situations, the manager removes obstacles from the path of talent. An advertising agency in San Francisco is impressive because it tapes a simple Latin motto to each of its managers' telephones: "NE SIM OBEX." Translated, it means "May I not be an obstacle." Employees working in this special kind of environment will inevitably approach their work in a more positive and productive way.

The need to change is here. Obviously, change means many challenges. It's a challenge for managers to instill that will to win, to get the juices flowing by putting employees on a marathon training schedule so that superior planning, strong management leadership, and a shared vision will enable them to win. It's a challenge for management to convince employees that they are the company; that they are not manual laborers but "validated" professionals operating with a sense of vision which gives them knowledge and decision-making power of their own; and that they are needed, wanted and respected. And it's a challenge for American corporations and companies to become customer driven—to make customers feel that the company understands them, and that the company's employees are on the customers' payrolls.

Accept the challenge, because as baseball great Yogi Berra said, "The future ain't what it used to be!"

10

PUT IT IN WRITING

By Warren Greshes

Warren Greshes is a professional speaker whose areas of expertise are sales and motivation. His audiences have included companies such as IBM, Sears, Allstate, BASF and Hertz. In particular, he focuses on commitment, goal-setting, self-motivation, customer service and sales. His focus is on teaching people how to motivate themselves to overcome the everyday roadblocks in life that make most people give up. Phone: 919-933-5900: e-mail: Greshes@mindspring.com.

You already know, have read, and/or been told that you should write down your goals. That writing down your goals is a valuable activity is not news to you. But, maybe the reason you've heard this advice so many times is because it's right!

Since you already know that you *should* write down your goals, I will provide you with additional information. When you've finished reading this chapter, you will know *why* you should write them down, and, even better, why they don't have to be "realistic" goals. In fact, I will demonstrate these certainties in ways that are so tangible and relevant to your everyday life that you'll no longer have an excuse not to establish your own goals.

WHY?

There are three excellent reasons why you should write down your goals.

The first reason is *so you won't forget them.* This falls under the category of "Things that sound dumb, but are true." But, haven't you ever awaken in the middle of the night with a good idea? What did you do? If you went back to sleep, undoubtedly that good idea was gone when you woke up the next morning. And be careful not to assume, "I won't forget my goals, they're much too important to me." That good idea you had was pretty important too. You were quite excited about it as you contemplated the millions you would make from that idea. Then you went back to sleep and four hours later it was forgotten. How long will it take you to forget your goals if you don't write them down?

The second reason you should write down your goals is that *writing down your goals is your first actual commitment* to achieving them. You have goals and dreams, including the big goals, the big dreams, the things you really want most out of life, which could take as much as two, three, five or more years of time, energy, effort and commitment to achieve. If you're not willing to take 10 minutes to write them down, what makes you think you'll be willing to put in years of effort and hard work to achieve them?

The third reason you should write down your goals is that *writing down your goals makes you accountable* to the one and only person you cannot fool—yourself. If you really wanted to, you could fool anyone. You could fool your spouse, children, parents, friends and coworkers. However, there's always one person who knows the absolute truth about you and your goals at all times: you. If you were to write down your goals, it would be hard to look at them and admit to yourself that you weren't willing to do everything it takes to get what you really wanted out of life. In fact, many people don't write down their goals because they do not really want to be accountable for them.

Now that I've identified why you should write down your goals, I'm going to keep my promise and demonstrate why you should get out your paper and pencil.

GROCERY STORE REVELATIONS

Have you ever done the grocery shopping for your household? While grocery shopping is a commonplace activity, doing it effectively requires a process remarkably similar to goal setting. Remember the times you have gone grocery shopping with a written list and those times you have gone without a list: What's the difference? Most people say they buy more groceries, spend more time and money, and forget things when they don't have a written shopping list. To paraphrase, when people carry out projects without written, focused directions and plans, they end up wasting time, wasting money, acquiring a lot of things they did not need and forgetting a lot of necessities. That last sentence applies to both grocery shopping and, as you've likely guessed, goal setting.

Did you ever notice when you go grocery shopping with a list how the shopping just seems to flow? You go aisle by aisle and before you know it, you're done. On the other hand, when you go without a list, you always seem to be running from one end of the store to the other. You grab something off a shelf, then realize you forgot something from the other end of the aisle. You can't say, "I'll get it later," because you're afraid if you don't do it now, you'll forget.

Without a list, you're likely to enter into supermarket deliberations. Standing in front of the peanut butter shelf, you say to yourself, "Do we have that? I'm sure we ran out. No, no, I think there's a couple of jars in cabinet. No I'm sure we ran out." Finally, you grab a jar off the shelf and say, "Oh what the hell, I'll buy a jar!" Then you get home only to find…three jars of peanut butter on the shelf.

Specifically, from surveys of the many audiences I've spoken to, the following are the results people observe when they go food shopping with and without lists:

WITH A LIST:

- It takes people about 10 minutes to write the shopping list;
- It takes about 1.5 hours to do the shopping (including round trip travel and bagging, loading and unloading the groceries).

WITHOUT A LIST:

- People spend about 30 minutes extra time shopping; and spend approximately $30 more than necessary.
- From this cumulative experience, we can summarize that the willingness to take 10 minutes at the beginning to develop a written, focused, direction and plan for something as simple as grocery shopping yielded these results within only an hour and a half (the time it takes to shop with a list):

    — A 30-minute savings or a 300 percent return on time invested;

    — Approximately $30 extra dollars in the pocket.

Imagine the yields if you applied the same principle to your life and career. That's why you write down your goals! The advantages of writing down your shopping list are the same ones you'll experience by writing down your life and career goals.

HOW TO WRITE THEM DOWN

Now that we've discussed the importance of putting your goals in writing, and you've pen in hand, let's examine the three components of a clearly defined, written goal.

BE SPECIFIC

It is not enough to say, "Next year I want to make to more money." Most people have vague goals. They talk in terms of, "a lot," "more," and "better." "I want to make a lot of money." "I want to live in a nicer house." "I'd like to have a better job." The problem with vague goals is that you can't formulate a plan to achieve them. When Olympic sprint and long-jump champion Carl Lewis sets a goal, he doesn't say, "I'd like to run faster or jump farther." He is specific about how much faster or how much farther because he must formulate a plan (or in his case, a training regimen) to achieve these increases.

What's "a lot" of money? Everyone's "a lot" is different; what's a lot to one person is not necessarily a lot to another. Yet it doesn't matter what your "a lot" is; what matters is that you know what it is so you can formulate a plan to achieve it.

Remember, it's only "a lot" if it's going to get you what you want. But if you don't know what you want, how do you know what you have to do to get it? And, if you don't know what it is, how will you know when you have it? When writing down your goals, please be specific.

DREAM WITH A DEADLINE

It's not enough to know what you want; you have to know by when. Time frames are critical when writing down your goals. They give you a frame of reference. After all, if you don't know when you plan to finish, what's the motivation to start? A goal scheduled "sometime" is doomed because "sometime" doesn't exist. We recognize the meaning of "sometime" in the following scenario:

You've run into someone you haven't seen in a while, and couldn't care less if you ever saw him or her again. You find yourself saying, "Hey, haven't seen you in ages. You look great! We should get together *sometime*. Give me a call *someday*. In fact, give me your number and I'll call you *sometime*." Why do you say that? Because you don't plan to see that person ever again.

When the time frame is "sometime," there is no real intention of accomplishing the goal.

FORGET ABOUT "REALISTIC"

The third component of writing down your goals requires that you place no limits on your ability to achieve. If it's what you really want, write it down. Don't ever put a glass ceiling over your head and rationalize your life away by saying, "This is what I really want, but I don't think I'll get it, so I'll settle for this." The second you say, "I'll settle," that's as far as you'll go.

One of my pet peeves is when I hear people say, "Set *realistic* goals." I don't believe in "realistic goals." To me, the word "realistic" is a code word. What it really means is, "low." When people say, "set realistic goals," what they mean is, "Set your goals so low that there'll be no way you can fail." What good is that? What good is setting a goal just because it's easy to achieve? If it's not what you really want, you're not going to be satisfied. In fact, by working for something you didn't even want, you'll just end up more frustrated. Your focus is no longer to succeed, but to avoid failure. Would you prefer to succeed or not fail?

When you ask someone just returning from ice-skating, "How was it?" he or she usually says something like, "I only fell once!" Big deal: If you hold on to the railing, you won't fall, but you're not really skating, either. Even professional skaters fall. If you want to be successful, you have to let go of the railing.

Dan Jansen, the Olympic gold medal speed-skater fell twice (1988 and 1992) in his quest for the gold medal. He obviously didn't fall because he was a lousy skater. Falling is a risk inherent to skating and in order to win the gold medal, he had to take risks, he had to skate to win. He couldn't skate just to not fall.

Every now and then, I meet someone who's out to prove me wrong. I remember once a young man came up to me and said, "You don't believe in realistic goals. OK, next year I want to make ten million dollars." My reply was, "Great! Who's stopping you." After all, lots of people in America have made ten million dollars in a year. "But first," I said, "let me tell you what you're going to have to do to earn that ten million dollars." When I had finished telling him everything he'd have to do, including all the time, energy, effort and commitment he'd have to put forth, he said, "Whoa, hold it; that's not very realistic." True, but it wasn't the ten million dollars that wasn't very realistic. What was unrealistic was his willingness to do what it took to make the ten million dollars.

Whether or not a goal is realistic is not determined by the goal, but rather by your willingness to do what it takes to achieve the goal. It's during the development of an action plan that reality sets in. After all, what's realistic? If a young boy or girl about 7 or 8 years old came up to you and said, "Someday I'm going to win a gold medal in the Olympics." Would you tell him or her to be "realistic" and not to aim so high. Many people would. But is it really unrealistic? It might be extremely difficult, but it's not unrealistic. Lots of people have won gold medals in the Olympics. However, an Olympic goal only becomes realistic if that young boy or girl is willing to dedicate him or herself daily to its accomplishment.

Dan Jansen practiced almost every day from the time he was 8 years old to achieve his goal of an Olympic gold medal. Olympic champions like Mary Lou Retton, Bonnie Blair and Carl Lewis gave up many of the pleasures and fun of adolescence to dedicate themselves to their "unrealistic goal." The great basketball legend, Larry Bird, a member of Dream Team I, the team that captured the 1992 Olympic gold medal in basketball, couldn't jump very high and was considered too slow to play professional basketball. His goal was definitely "unrealistic." But he was always the first person to arrive at practice and the last to leave. He never stopped "doing what it takes" to achieve his goal.

Who's to decide what's realistic and what isn't? We know from experience that people can accomplish amazing things when they put their minds to it. After all, if a young girl would have come up to you 25 years ago and said, "I'm going to be one of the biggest stars in the world and I'm going to do it by wearing my underwear outside my clothes." You would have said, "Now that's unrealistic." But that young girl became Madonna and not only did she become one of the biggest stars in the world, but she started a new fashion craze by wearing her underwear outside her clothes.

Remember there's no goal that's unrealistic, only people who aren't willing to do what it takes to achieve those "unrealistic" goals.

11

HOW TO BE AN OLYMPIC ROAD WARRIOR

by Jeff Davidson, MBA, CMC

An authority on living and working at a comfortable pace, Jeff Davidson is the award-winning author of 18 books which have been selected by 20 book clubs and published in nine languages. His 18th and most widely acclaimed book, *Breathing Space: Living and Working at a Comfortable Pace in a Sped-Up Society*, has been translated into Chinese, Italian, Malay and Spanish. A full-time speaker since January 1994, his presentations focus on personal performance, profitability, organizational excellence, productivity, stress-reduction and balance. Phone: 919-932-1995; e-mail: Jeff@BreathingSpace.com; web site: www.BreathingSpace.com.

For an Olympic athlete, staying fit is a prerequisite to performing well on the field. For too many business executives and career professionals staying fit is an onerous task, and much more so while traveling.

As your work load begins to pile up it's easy to start skipping exercise. It's also easy to rationalize when traveling that if your normal exercise routines have been disrupted, you can wait until you get back home before resuming them. This kind of thinking led me to a weight of 201 pounds in two years after having maintained a trim 178 to 182 for 23 years!

Fortunately, I'm back down to 180 pounds, and I did it in a six-month period. In addition, I did it without any hunger cravings, diet pills, total sacrifices, or extreme physical exertion. Here are the key components that enabled me not only to regain the body that I wanted, but to get into even better shape than I had been before.

DO SOME KIND OF EXERCISE EVERYDAY

I learned a valuable tip from a friend who I noticed was trim and toned. He said that he made it a rule to exercise at least some portion of each day, even if it was just a 15-minute walk around the block.

Some exercise each day is more than just a challenge for your body, it becomes an intellectual challenge whereby you actively devise ways to work out in otherwise confining conditions. Suppose you're stuck in a small city, in a small hotel with no athletic facilities, and there's a thundering rainstorm outside. The challenge becomes using the hotel's hallways, or even your own hotel room as your "gym."

HOTEL ROOM AS HEALTH CLUB

When you check into your hotel, always ask for a nonsmoking room on a nonsmoking floor. You get your best exercise in rooms in which nicotine has not infiltrated the carpets and curtains. Also ask if the hotel has a health club, pool, or other type of exercise facility. If it does, great. If not, it's relatively simple to use your hotel room for your workout.

When I check into hotels I often ask if a second- or third-floor room is available (If there's a fire I could jump or climb from the window). Staying on lower floors prompts me to walk more often than I otherwise would—I feel guilty when I take the elevator just to go up a floor or two. Walking up and down stairs is an excellent exercise that gives a good workout to muscles in your back, derriere and legs. I don't recommend using the stairs when you're toting luggage, but once you put the luggage down, use the stairs as often as you can.

When it comes to television in the hotel or at home, I have a personal rule: I never watch a sporting contest without being engaged in some kind of activity myself. For example, if I'm watching 24-year-old NBA basketball players run up and down the court, I simultaneously run in place, do arm circles, or squats. If you've ever taken an aerobics class, you know many exercises that you can perform in a 4-foot square space.

If watching sports is not your thing, you can undertake the same type of exercises while watching a movie, perhaps a pay-per-view movie, the length of which you know exactly, and hence the length of your workout. Half-hour shows and one-hour shows work just as well. If you agree with Bruce Springsteen, "57 channels and nothing on," simply take the remote control in one hand and keep flicking the dial as you run in place or do some other kind of calisthenics. Or, you could always flip on the radio, find an appropriate station, and exercise to the beat of the music.

When do you exercise in your hotel room? Not just when you're pent up because of bad weather, but anytime you feel like it. Sometimes, after a long flight, I'll take a quick 20-minute nap. Then I'll get up and exercise in front of a TV show for 30 minutes, take a shower, and be ready for the rest of the day or evening. Surprisingly, by working out in front of the television for as little as 30 minutes, you're much more energized to walk around the grounds or the city.

If 30 or 60 minutes of calisthenics or running in place sounds like too much for you, simply do stretches during that time—perhaps yoga would be enjoyable for you. There are several good books available, most with plenty of illustrations and diagrams to show you the basic yoga stretches.

Bring your golf ball

One of the things I always carry with me when I travel is a golf ball. With shoes and socks off, and the golf ball on the floor, roll each foot slowly over the golf ball. Doing this can relieve tension in various parts of your body. Reflexologists have long told us that the bottom of each foot is a map of pressure points to all other parts of the body; reflexology is a fairly complex system. In essence, the pressure of the ball on certain areas of your foot triggers responses in corresponding parts of the body.

Those places where the underside of your foot is tender correspond to those places in the body that are currently weak or stressed. Even though the pressure from the ball hurts, continue to gently roll your foot over the ball, back and forth, until that pain begins to subside a little. Then switch to the other foot. This technique works well in hotel rooms because they're virtually all carpeted.

If you undertake this activity on successive days, you'll begin to notice that any pain felt on the underside of your feet tends to diminish. This is a good sign indeed, for it means the corresponding part of your body is less stressed and getting stronger.

Hotel health club

If the hotel has a health club, then you have far more tools at your disposal. I find the treadmills and bike machines to be great for warm-ups because in each case you can start at slow speed. If the health club facility has mirrors along the walls, forget about narcissism and face the mirror while you exercise. This will help you maintain your form, and may prompt you to stay on the bike or machine longer or do more repetitions of whatever it is you're doing.

While exercising on the road, I try to keep any health club workout light. This is not the time to try to break your endurance record on the bike machines, or lift the maximum number of times, or venture into new weight levels you haven't attempted before. I recommend staying within 60 to 70 percent of your optimal performance levels while on the road. If the health club facility has a sauna, steam room, or whirlpool bath, feel free to use them—but don't overdo it. Prolonged stays in any of these can actually drain energy from you.

When the hotel has no health club facility

Walk the halls or, if the weather is favorable, the grounds of the hotel facility. In many cases, a couple times around the block will give you 15 minutes of solid walking. If you're near a supermarket or neighborhood shopping center—or better yet, a large shopping mall—you can easily spend an hour walking up and down the aisles and hallways. Don't linger too much to look at the goods; your goal is to stay in motion.

Sometimes as I walk along at a brisk pace, I swing my arms vigorously. It looks funny to others, but the cardiovascular system responds well to such activity. If you can raise your arms above your head and perhaps swing them as you walk, you'll give your cardiovascular system a good workout. Orchestra conductors live longer than average men and women. It's postulated that all that time waving their batons above heart level strengthens their heart muscles.

Airports as playgrounds

Suppose you have a layover in an airport for an hour and 45 minutes. The challenge becomes to use that airport as your playing field. Inevitably, you'll have layovers in the course of your travels. When I know in advance I'm going to be spending some time in airports, I undertake steps to ensure that I'll be free and unencumbered during that time, so I can walk up and down the hallways of these clean, smoke-free, well-ventilated structures.

Sometimes, after I check my largest bags, I take off (depending on how much time I have) for the far ends of the airport. Usually I've got on sneakers or walking shoes, as I've already packed my business shoes. One time, I was delayed in a Cincinnati airport for two hours and 40 minutes, and because of the extremely long walking path, was able to get a two-hour and 15-minute workout by going up and back only twice. Airports have great advantages for walkers as there are water fountains, bathrooms, and lots of people and shops to view. This is particularly true at the Pittsburgh airport where there's now a huge shopping mall right in the midst of everything.

DRINK WATER

Water is an important part of weight reduction. When you're exhausted, you often really need water more than sleep. Drinking a nice glass of water can keep you active longer. When you're in a shopping mall and feel the need to sit down, take a seat if you have to, but first look for a water fountain. A drink may be enough to rejuvenate you and prompt you to walk for another 10 or 15 minutes. Before meals, drinking a glass or two of water will not only aid in digestion and elimination, but will reduce the overall volume of food you ingest.

Yes, drinking more water will result in more frequent urination, but that's good too. Most of us don't drink enough in the course of the day, and traveling in airplanes is particularly dehydrating. Medical experts say that you need an 8-ounce glass of water for every hour in flight.

Too many people choose soda, coffee and other drinks as a means of getting the fluid they need. Don't mess with the rest; water is the best. When I travel, I always bring my own 10-ounce water bottle. Rather than wait for the flight attendants to bring drinks, or scramble over people and walking down a crowded aisle to get water, I have it available at my seat for drinking whenever I choose. This can make all the difference as to whether you arrive refreshed or beat.

THE PLANE AS YOUR EXERCISE ROOM

If you're on a jumbo-jet plane with double aisles, walking isn't a problem. You can probably walk up and down one of the aisles, cutting across as bottle necks occur. Stay on your feet a good five or ten minutes without irritating the flight attendants. If you're on a single-aisle plane, take at least one walk for every 45 minutes in flight up and down the aisle, even if only to go to the restroom.

I've found that in the back of the plane, there's usually more room to do some light stretches, deep-knee bends, quick arm motions and the like. The flight attendants understand and it doesn't really upset any passengers. It might look funny and it might feel funny, but it's your trip, your career, your body and your weight. Get into some stretching while you're on the plane, and you'll have energy and endurance when you're on the ground. It will help you maintain and regain your fighting weight.

WALK—DON'T EAT—AFTER 7 P.M.

By not eating after 7 p.m., I've experienced a profound change in my life. The later you eat in the day, the less efficiently your body digests and assimilates what you've eaten. Eating late at night can also lead you to awaken with a sluggish feeling in the morning. I eat as much as I want for dinner, but conclude before 7 p.m. as often as possible. This schedule creates an almost 12-hour fast. After dinner, I usually try to take a walk. Instead of taking in more calories after 7 p.m., you're burning them. The net result is that in as little as two or three months you will begin to see great results.

You may be thinking, "But, I'll be famished at 9 or 10 in the evening." Actually, this is not the case. Often, I'll just sip a glass of water, especially those nights when I retire early. Then I'll wake up, have a good breakfast, and feel fit and raring to go.

BREAKING THE CYCLE

When you work out vigorously for hours on end as so many people in health clubs do, you fall into a cycle that's hard to sustain. The cycle includes overcompensating for:

- Dehydration (so you fill up on water),
- Hunger (so you fill up on food),
- Weariness.

Fatigue and exhaustion from vigorous workouts may lead to overeating and disturbed sleep routines. When you simply walk, do calisthenics in front of the TV, and pursue other methods of light exercise, you never get into the dehydration, hunger, and tiredness cycle. In fact, I was able to drop 21 pounds with no hunger cravings whatsoever, and with no tiredness. It felt natural, it was relatively easy, and now I don't know how I ever let myself balloon up to 201 in the first place.

With my regained energy, I'm playing basketball with the 18- to 24-year olds again, and walking the historic part of cities where I'm speaking. All my clothes fit well. People routinely take me for someone several years younger. I feel great.

A GOOD NIGHT'S SLEEP ON THE ROAD

An important element to success when you're on the road is getting a good night's sleep. Whether you're an athlete, business executive, or career professional, undoubtedly you know the value of getting good sleep. All too often, however, as you bed down for the night in a hotel the guest from hell is in the next room attempting to break the decibel barrier with the TV volume at 2:30 a.m. Even if you're normally a sound sleeper, you should take precautions to ensure a good night's sleep every night.

YOU CAN ALWAYS CALL THE MANAGER

If noise is invading the space you've rented and it's easy to determine that the source of the sound is from an adjacent room to the left or right, you could try tapping on the wall. This alone sometimes works. In many hotels, the phone system allows you to readily dial adjacent rooms. If the noise is from across the hall or above or below you, you could also, of course, call the night manager and ask him or her to handle the situation. Usually the night manager will ring the room or send up a security officer to tap on the door and take care of the situation face-to-face.

I don't recommend that you leave your hotel room to directly address the offender(s). You never know how strangers are going to react to being told they're making too much noise, and it's not really your place to confront anyone directly. It is the hotel's responsibility since the cost of the room rental includes the explicit or implicit promise of quiet enjoyment.

CREATE WHITE NOISE

If you've been wakened and the offending noise isn't too outrageous, use the TV or radio to create white noise. With the TV, select a channel that emits a static sound and turn the brightness down to nothing, or cover the entire set with a blanket or towel to minimize any light coming from the TV. Be sure to position it between you and the source of the noise. In many instances, the TV's muffled static sound will be enough to block the more offensive noise.

The same principle works with the radio. As you seek a suitable position along the radio dial, make sure you're not near any signal that might get stronger during the night, otherwise you may defeat your purpose.

Experiment with your room's thermostat. Perhaps you can turn on the fan, or the heating or cooling system, depending on the season. Use the ventilation system as a white noise device and then adjust the number of blankets and sheets you need accordingly. Using the ventilation system is often effective for muffling sounds above or below your room.

Use your own alarm clock

On the road, use your own alarm clock, or better yet, timer. By setting your own timer, you can wake up on cue after having unplugged your room telephone for the night.

When you remove the plug from the telephone, be sure to position the cord so that the end is exposed to you; it will serve as a reminder in the morning to reconnect the phone.

Preventive Measures While Checking In

- Explain to the check-in staff that getting good sleep is crucial. This alone might prompt them to give you a room that is known to be in a quiet section of the hotel.

- Specifically ask for a room where you'll have peace and quiet. In general, these are rooms away from elevators, or opposite the street side or front of the hotel.

- Ask for a room without a door adjoining another room, where the guest from hell is likely to be staying.

12

BUSINESS OLYMPICS: GOLD MEDAL CUSTOMER SERVICE

by Shep Hyken, C.S.P.

Shep Hyken is professional speaker and author who has been entertaining audiences with his unique presentation style for 24 years. Also a magician, in 1983 he made the transition from entertainer to speaker. He mixes information with entertainment as he speaks on his most requested topics: customer service, internal service and customer relations. His clients include American Airlines, Anheuser-Busch, AT&T, Fleming Foods, General Motors, Holiday Inn, Kraft, Monsanto, Shell Oil and Standard Oil. Phone: 314-692-2200; e-mail: Shep@hyken.com; web site: www.hyken.com.

Achieving Gold Medal Customer Service involves more than just taking care of your customers. You must exceed all of their expectations. It takes more than just satisfying your customers. You must make them want to come back again and again.

Delivering gold medal customer service takes a team of dedicated people, performing at the optimum level, to produce the gold for an organization. And with that gold comes the reward of getting and keeping the customer. As simple as the concept is, there are a number of factors involved in performing at the gold level of customer service.

So how can you and your organization achieve the gold medal in customer service? There is no such thing as a Business Olympics. Or, is there? Many companies have supplier/vendor programs that recognize and reward top performance. However, the closest thing to a business Olympics might be the Malcolm Baldrige Quality Award, sponsored by United States Department of Commerce. This award is given to organizations that excel in many areas of business, with an emphasis on delivering excellent customer service. When you win the Malcolm Baldrige Quality Award you have won the gold medal in the Business Olympics. And, even though the award is intangible—a title and some prestige—the secondary reward, incredibly happy customers who buy again and again, is invaluable.

This is not to suggest that your organization attempt to win the Malcolm Baldrige Quality Award. Just completing the application takes lots of time and money. To achieve gold medal customer service an organization does not need to submit its application; its members simply need to perform—or outperform—the award's customer service standards. Tremendous time and effort have gone into creating the requirements to win the award, and these requirements can become the benchmark and goals your organization needs to begin providing gold medal customer service.

CORPORATE IDOLS

Personal idols inspire us to reach and expand our goals. The same holds true in the competition of business. If you want a business idol, look to the winners of the Malcolm Baldrige Quality Award. These winners, along with their leaders, can be our corporate idols. Some of the more recognizable winners include Federal Express, IBM, Cadillac, AT&T, GTE, Ritz Carlton, Texas Instruments and Xerox. These are some of our corporate heroes, and unlike some of the famous sports legends, they are very accessible. The Malcolm Baldrige Award winners have published their entire applications with additional information that will get you well on your way to understanding what goes on behind their gold medal performances. All you have to do to get this information is to contact:

> Malcolm Baldrige National Quality Award
> National Institute of Standards and Technology
> Administration Building, Room A
> Gaithersburg, MD 20899-0001
> PHONE: (301) 975-2036

To get into the race of the Business Olympics means getting into the real business world. It means competing with other businesses, domestic and international, for the same top honor: a customer's business. The judges are not former athletes and coaches from the sport. They are CEOs, VPs, purchasing departments, consumers, etc.; anyone who buys or would potentially buy, our products and services. The winners are awarded the business by these judges.

So how can your organization convince these "judges" that you are the best?

WHAT IS CUSTOMER SERVICE?

Many businesses define service as the sales process or the follow-through of the sales process. Some organizations even assign customer service its own department. This couldn't be further from the truth! Service is neither a department nor a part of the sales process. Customer service is an attitude that everyone within an organization must have. It is with this attitude and a team spirit toward winning over and keeping customers that an organization can achieve gold medal customer service.

In planning a service strategy, the goal is to build long-term relationships with your customers. It's important not only to get new customers into our businesses, but to focus on getting the new customers to come back again and again. Dr. Theodore Levitt, Senior Professor at Harvard Business School, says getting and keeping customers is the main *function* of a business. However, many businesses assume their function is to make a profit. Making a profit is actually the *goal* of the business. If you confuse the function with the goal, you may not reach the goal. Remember, winning in this arena means winning the customer. The benefit of winning the customer potentially means profit.

In most Olympic sports, it takes more than one try to earn a gold medal. An athlete may win one event, but then must go on to compete in others to achieve the world-class title. This is no different in business. Customer service is just part of a total customer-satisfaction program and a key to getting and keeping the customer. Service alone will not make a business successful. Other areas such as product selection, business location, advertising, etc., are vital. But in many cases, excellent service will compensate for other competitive problems such as pricing issues.

GOLD MEDAL EXPECTATIONS

To begin planning for gold medal service it is important to put together a program. This program must involve everyone in your organization. While all members of the organization may not be dealing directly with outside customers, they have internal customers (other members of the organization) who must be satisfied. Everything discussed here applies to both the internal and external customer.

Let's start with understanding what customers expect. Customers expect quality in all areas of the business—not just in service! While employees have to deliver service, the quality of our products and image of our business must also be considered.

Customers expect businesses to *solve problems*. Businesses, in addition to selling, are expected to be experts in their respective fields. Businesses are expected to fulfill product needs as well as answer any questions customers might have. In addition, businesses are expected to solve problems that become complaints. Recovery from complaints can often be the single most important factor in keeping your organization in the game.

Customers expect *speed*. With so much competition in the game of business, there are a few things that can set you apart. Excellent service helps, and in many cases speed helps even more. We're talking about speed in delivery, handling problems, returning phone calls, processing orders-speed in virtually all aspects of the business.

Customers expect *consistency*. You can't be great one day, and average the next. Think about a time you may have gone to a restaurant and had an excellent meal, only to return and have an average experience at best. Gold medal organizations don't get where they are with inconsistent service. They may have bad days, but they recover so well that it doesn't matter. Their recovery is consistent with their original goal: to obtain (or renew) the confidence of the customer.

Customers expect *reliability* and *dependability*. A relationship of confidence and trust needs to be established. The customer needs this confidence not only in the business, but in the personnel as well. Deliver on all of their expectations, and you will be deemed reliable and dependable by your customers.

Customers expect *acknowledgment*. Customers need to know that they are making the right decision in doing business with you. Acknowledgment comes in the form of "Thank yous." Dr. Larry Baker says, "The most abused customer is the sold customer." Let customers know how much you appreciate their business. Let your inside customers know how much you appreciate their hard work and dedication to the team. A survey taken by Robert Half International indicated that the number one reason an employee will leave a company to work for someone else is lack of recognition and acknowledgment for his or her work. Consider thank you notes, maybe even birthday or holiday cards. These go a long way in building loyalty, inside and out.

Understanding that meeting and exceeding expectations will get you closer to the gold is just a first step. Now you need a strategy to get you there. The strategy is as simple and basic as building the strongest relationship possible with your customer. The following are five ways to help build stronger relationships with your customers and get you closer to winning the gold.

IMPRESSIONS

Managing impressions is of prime importance. The moment a customer has any contact with your business he or she should have a positive experience. Everything from the physical layout of the business to an employee's approach to the customer has an effect on the impressions made during this contact. This contact is known as the "Moment of Truth."

Jan Carlzon, former president of Scandinavian Air, says the Moment of Truth is "anytime a customer comes into contact with any aspect of a business, however remote, and has an opportunity to form an impression." How you manage these moments of truth is what makes or breaks careers and businesses. These moments of truth can be good, average or bad. Your goal should be to manage all moments of truth so well that gold medal performance is always delivered. All opportunities must be considered, from the physical appearance of a business, the professionalism of all personnel, to the advertising you use to promote the business.

Also realize that these impressions are ongoing and that many more than just first impressions must be managed. Every time you walk into a meeting, you create an impression that will affect the outcome of that meeting. How do people perceive you when you answer the phone? The way you answer the phone could prove disastrous. Or, it could be the beginning of a positive conversation. There is a lot more to managing impressions than simply the first time someone walks through your doors. Every contact is a moment of truth and an opportunity to make a gold impression.

KNOWLEDGE OF THE BUSINESS

Knowledge is crucial to building a relationship and meeting the customer's needs. Specifically, knowledge of the business can be divided into two parts: knowledge of your business/industry and knowledge of the customer. Gold medalists will be sought out as authorities and sources of knowledge within their business. Others will not be consulted.

Pertaining to knowledge of your business and industry, if your employees are trained to be experts in their fields, their ongoing ability to provide answers and solve the customer's problems is one of the strongest ways to build a long term relationship. Employees need to know about the latest, the greatest and the state-of-the-art. They need to know as much as possible about the competition. Wouldn't it be nice if your customers called your company every time they had a question relating to what it is that you sell—even if it was about the competition?

Knowledge of the customer means knowing as much as you possibly can about your customer. You need to know more than just the name, what department and place of employment. You need to know about his or her spouse or significant other. You need to find out about children, hobbies and the family dog. People love it when you take interest in them. In Harvey Mackay's book, *Swim With the Sharks Without Being Eaten Alive,* he talks about the Mackay 66. These are 66 questions you should have answered regarding each of your customers in order to know your customer very well.

GENERAL KNOWLEDGE

Know a little bit about a lot of things. That means being a well-rounded person. You need to talk to people on a level beyond business. Know what is happening in your community and the world. Read newspapers and magazines. Watch the news at night. Be able to move your relationship away from business to a more personal level. This will go a long way in building stronger relationships.

ENTHUSIASM

Enthusiasm is important. Some enthusiasm may be generated by employee motivational programming, but overall, it has to be characteristic of the person in the first place. Many companies are beginning to consider the attitude of a potential employee more important than his or her aptitude. If you are not excited about what you do, how can you excite the customer enough to want to do business with you, and more importantly, continue to want to do business with you? You must be enthusiastic! Enthusiasm is contagious. Danny Cox, a famous business speaker, says, "If enthusiasm is contagious, then anything you have that is not enthusiasm is also contagious."

THINKING LIKE YOUR CUSTOMER

This means understanding what your customers want and need—sometimes even better than they do. It means doing it right the first time every time—no mistakes. It means consistently delivering a performance of a perfect 10. You can't do this if you don't understand your customers.

You may assume that you know what your customers want when, in reality, they want something else. You can avoid this mistake simply by taking the time to ask the right questions and clarify the answers. Then you can be sure that you are delivering what your customers want and need.

TRAINING FOR CUSTOMER SERVICE

Now it is time to start training with this program. You understand a customer's expectations, and you have five relationship-building skills to meet and exceed them. You must practice these skills, but not all at once. Here is a five-day training program that should be repeated every week until these concepts become natural to you and your employees. At the end of each day, write down at least three examples of when you used each of the following skills.

Monday is "Gold Impression Day." Be aware of every contact with a customer. Especially note when you are making a positive first impression. Be aware of every opportunity to make both you and your company shine.

Tuesday is "Knowledge of Your Business Day." Throughout the day, demonstrate that you are an expert in your field. If you have people working for you make sure you are constantly feeding them new and useful information. Try to use and share brand new information that you may have learned recently. Use this knowledge of your business to assure people, giving them additional confidence that they are dealing with the right people and the right organization. Use information you know about your customers to help illustrate that you have taken the extra step to get to know them on a personal as well as professional level.

Wednesday is "General Knowledge Day." Wednesday is your day to build stronger relationships by talking about other people's interests.

Whether you are talking about something from the morning paper, politics or a famous literary work, try to build a personal rapport with your customers.

Thursday is the day of "Enthusiasm." On this day you must stay "up" and motivated about your responsibilities to your organization and its customers. While you should be excited about what you do all of the time, push yourself extra hard and you will be amazed at the impact you will have on others.

Friday is "Understand Your Customer Day." Be aware that asking the right questions can give your customers what they want, versus what it is that you think that they want. Recognize that a potential misunderstanding can be overcome by truly understanding your customer's wants, needs and desires.

Repeat this training program week after week. Just to say you are going to take care of customers more effectively is not the answer. You have to plan and train. If you take this five-day approach and keep a written log of your accomplishments throughout each day, eventually you won't even have to think to make these skills work for you. This is no different from the athlete who works and trains to develop muscle memory. What you are developing is "service memory."

Service can be measured and results tracked over a period of time. You can't get into the Olympics overnight. You have to work and train. Starting tomorrow won't get your old customers back or guarantee your new customers will stay. But, it is a start. Train your staff and practice these techniques day in and day out. This cannot be a part-time effort. It needs to be implemented in every facet of your organization, and it needs to stay there.

Your company is a team, organized to win. In a tough competitive business environment, excellent service is one of your most powerful assets. The customers are the judges and your prize is their business.

13

THE MAGIC OF MAGNETIC IMAGERY

by James E. Melton, Ph.D.

James Melton has a varied background as a journalist, college instructor and commercial pilot. He has a Ph.D. in management and has written two best-selling books. Also he has developed the Melton Learning System, a video-based training series. He is recognized as a modern philosopher as he travels the globe sharing insights on achieving higher levels of personal and professional success. PBS has produced a series on his work entitled "Reaching New Heights of Excellence." He is a frequent guest on national radio and television talk shows. Phone: 760-323-4204; e-mail: Info@4speakers.com; web site: www.4speakers.com.

Paging through the newspaper during the summer the Olympics were held in Los Angeles, I was struck by one page that stood out in sparkling, energized color. A time-lapsed photo of a pole vaulter displayed the athlete in the first stage of springing himself into the air. The fiberglass pole was bowed to the maximum. His sleek, muscular body was lifting from the ground into the air. This entire full-page photo held but one single caption, "A lifetime of training for eight seconds of flight."

What makes an Olympic athlete? What makes some people strive for such great achievements? In reality, most people have the physical ability to achieve greatness. The one factor that blocks them is the lack of self-discipline and mental direction. Let's talk about how to prepare your mind for greatness. But first we have to prepare the body.

Any Olympic athlete knows that keeping the body in tune is essential. Most people perform preventive maintenance on their car. Those that do change the oil about every three or four thousand miles, change the oil filter, get a tune-up every now and then, and rotate the tires. They generally maintain the automobile in such a manner to minimize the chance that problems will occur at inappropriate times. If people would spend as much time and thought on the vehicle that walks them around as they do on the vehicle that drives them around, it's a sure bet they would be in much better shape.

LISTEN TO YOUR BODY

When your car is in desperate need of oil you don't drive it for another 300 or 400 miles before adding the oil. You know that if you do not fill the tank with gas when it's low, you will not be going much farther. When the tires get bald, it would be senseless to begin a long journey without getting some tread under you. The body, on the other hand, may cry out for a certain kind of food which is denied because its owner is too busy to eat, or is trying to lose weight quickly. It may be in desperate need of rest or even sleep, but is prohibited by an overly crowded schedule. However, if these messages are not heard, the body will make itself heard by giving us even louder messages.

The louder message may come, for example, in the form of a sore throat. The body says, "Can you hear this?" But if you don't give it much thought and go to work anyway, the body will start to raise its voice—you develop a cold and possibly a cough. The voice will get louder and louder until finally you will have to listen, thereby changing your thinking and working patterns to accommodate the illness with corrective measures.

INSIDE YOUR HEAD

Now, let's talk about mental conditioning. If you are not experiencing what you want in any area, it is absolutely imperative that you change your basic trend of thought. Whatever situation is foremost on your mind, whether you think it has anything to do with your illness or not, change it. Or better yet, don't think about it at all. This is difficult, but it is imperative that you change your basic trend of thought.

How do you do this? Follow this example: Think of something unpleasant (this should not be too difficult because that's what most people think about anyway). Hold the thought for a moment.

Now, switch your attention to a rose garden. It is outside and the roses have a fragrance that fills the air. Reach down and smell an individual rose. In your mind, feel the softness of its petals, their silky smoothness. What color is your rose? Be careful of the thorns on the stem for they are quite sharp; handle them gently. A fresh bouquet of roses in the home is food for the mind and spirit.

What happened to the unpleasant thought? When you thought of the rose, you could not think of something unpleasant. You can replace one thought with another. It takes constant practice. A trend of thinking will struggle to maintain its own existence. It is possible only to observe the thoughts as they go by, without judgment, without planning future thoughts. Now, in this present moment, a rose is a rose. This moment is all you can manage, especially during trying circumstances such as relationship problems, deteriorating health, or financial collapse. After all, things like these are common, everyday events that tend to keep people from achieving their dreams. The Olympic athlete also faces similar daily challenges. How do they succeed?

One reason is that they are able to switch their attention from one thought to another. So can you. When you are redirecting your thoughts, do this with a relaxed body. Loosen your muscles; ease up a bit. One of John F. Kennedy's greatest attributes was his ability to leave a meeting and enter another meeting on an entirely different subject, and give it his 100 percent attention.

WHAT YOU SEE IS WHAT YOU GET

The old saying is especially true when dealing with the mind. A variation could also be stated: "What you see is what you become." Experimental and clinical psychologists have proved that the mind cannot tell the difference between an actual physical visual impression and one imagined, vividly and in detail. Since we all think in pictures and feelings, your inherent tendency to visualize will continually produce images as you read this essay.

Understanding reduces the complex to the simple. By understanding the workings of your own mental camera, you will be able to focus on your desires and bring them into your own physical reality. There is a certain basic way in which we think of ourselves. The pattern of thought or belief that you have about yourself is carried with you and colors your entire experience.

WHEREVER I GO, THERE I AM

I know a man who, for a long while, lived in New York. Things were going quite badly for him. Money was not coming in, his wife turned against him, his friends seemed to drift away, and in general, he was having a bad time of it. He got the idea to move. After giving it some thought, he packed up and went to Chicago, looking for that fresh start, that new beginning, the new life he had heard about.

Chicago offered new challenges, and he met them—using the same methods he used in New York. His financial situation did not improve, he seemed to make only acquaintances, not friends, and in short, he felt like he was still living in New York.

Thinking that a warmer climate would solve his problems, off he went to California—balmy breezes, sun and fun. He met a fine young woman, established a business, and began the pattern again. This woman, too, left him and the business was another financial disaster. Why? Because wherever he went he took himself along! When you want to change anything, from health, to business; from relationships, to finances, you have to leave the old you behind and move forward in the new direction with a new attitude. You have to see yourself in your mind as being a different person. To do this, you must exercise the power of your mental camera.

Focus in

What I am describing is forming imagery patterns of your desire in your mind, crystallizing images on your mind, taking mental photographs of things yet unseen in the physical world. This is not magic. It is simply the way the mind works.

Thinking is the beginning of forming an image on the film of your mind. A really sharp image is ideal, but acquiring one may take some practice. We all imprint our minds with imagery of amazing clarity by dreams and our fantasies. This process is called hypnagogic imagery, or creative imagery. The mind travels through a hypnagogic state just prior to falling asleep. Once you learn to relax the body completely without falling asleep you will be able to experience this type of imagery. You will clearly see patterns, scenes, people, usually common ordinary images, not at all intertwined with the symbols which often occur in dreams. By remaining unemotional when these images come into your mind, you can retain them and experience this vivid imagery as a comparison to your own predetermined mental pictures.

How do you feel?

Imagery is a valuable tool to develop a feeling. The body responds to feelings as well as to pictures, and if you really have a gut feeling of health, prosperity, success, love, caring or leadership, you will exemplify that trait. If you do not have an extremely strong feeling of your desire, through mental imagery, a definite feeling cannot be developed.

Through imagery you can tune into your inner senses. You can use an image of what you want but do not yet have, to obtain what you want. To achieve health, wealth and happiness, for example, you may turn to the physically unseen. By clicking the shutter of your mind and forming a series of mental pictures of your desire, you establish harmonious vibration with that desire and set into motion the laws of attraction which draw to you the physical counterpart of your idea, your thought.

PLANTING THE SEED

The analogy that ideas are like seeds is useful. It takes time to grow seeds into mature trees, flowers or vegetables. It also takes plenty of sunlight, water, and proper attention. The same is true with an infant. A baby needs attention, watering, feeding, changing, love, warmth, holding, compassion, understanding, and more. A neglected child can not be expected to grow; it takes time and nourishing to "grow" a healthy child.

Mental seeds are planted by forming a picture of our desire in our mind. If results are not reaped immediately, we should not condemn the seed and say, "This doesn't work." Patience is necessary.

TRANSMUTATION

You cannot escape the results of your thoughts. You are not what you want, you are what you think and believe. You will realize the vision in your mind, not the idle wish. A vision held frequently and firmly will tend to manifest itself more quickly than one held in the mind only occasionally. Frequency and intensity will be very important in making your dream a reality. Just as the seed planted in the ground requires time to grow, so does a vision need a gestation or incubation period.

There is no set time period necessary to manifest a vision. However, the speed with which change occurs is directly related to the frequency with which one thinks about a vision and the degree of one's emotional involvement in a vision. Frequency and intensity are two key factors in bringing your true heart's desire into reality. Most people plant the seed and then fluctuate in their response and intensity. From expectancy (looking for results in the first hour, day, or week) and excitement, they swing between doubt, hope, and wishing. From sureness, firmness, and affirmation, they default to concern, despair, and uncertainty. Then follows a period of re-excitement, interest, and enthusiasm, perhaps succeeded by a new period of fear, anger, and depression.

And so it goes, back and forth. More often than not, too much vacillation prevents an individual from getting his or her heart's desire. It's not that the vision wasn't any good (remember, the mind does not judge visions), it's because he or she bounced back and forth between confidence and defeat. For every contradictory thought sustained, the time necessary for the desired change to take place is extended. If you plant weeds along with your crop of visions, the harvest becomes a jumbled mess, and sometimes even the sprouting seedlings cannot be recognized. A farmer doesn't go out each day to dig up the seed to see if it has grown!

DESTRUCTIVE, PASSIVE, AGGRESSIVE

Magnetic imagery will always attract a corresponding environment to you. The rate at which your visual image becomes reality is adjustable. Because of this, the method by which you form your mental pictures becomes extremely important.

Picture your desired end results in terms of a present possibility. For example, let's say you are informed of a possible delay in returning home from a business trip, and you don't want to be home late. A procedure to follow could be picturing yourself returning home, greeting the family and turning on the 5 o'clock news, confirming that you arrived home safely and on time. This is called passive imagery, and it will certainly have some effect. However, it is not a very dynamic mental picture. Although it is possible to frequently picture this in your mind, you may have a little trouble getting the necessary intensity behind it to bring it into reality. An example of destructive imagery would be to see and feel yourself not arriving on time, not beating the traffic, and not succeeding.

Now, take the same situation (keeping in mind that you really want to be there) and picture this: As you open the door to your home you are hit by the tantalizing aroma of roasted duck l'orange. You close the door behind you and the old grandfather's clock right in front of you strikes five. The room is dimly lit by candles; the table is set for two. As your wife turns off the 5 o'clock news, she comes over to you, puts her arms around you and says, "I'm so glad you're home on time, Honey; I have planned a special dinner just for us tonight." Can you see the difference? This last example qualifies as aggressive magical imagery.

Both passive and aggressive imagery can be effective, but aggressive imagery brings into play all the senses—sight, sound, taste, smell and touch. The "on-time" sequence was reinforced three times—by the clock, by the TV and by the wife. It is possible to achieve both frequency and intensity with the aggressive mental picture.

Another example of mental imagery might be the following. Imagine that you want an area cleared and a hole dug for a swimming pool. Your daughter or son may be preparing for the Olympics and you want to do everything you can in support. You have men working on it, but progress is slow. You may be picturing the men doing their jobs, but in a very passive and lazy way, thereby causing progress to continue at a slow pace. At this rate, it will be completed eventually, but you want your Olympic prospect to be able to use the pool as soon as possible. Use aggressive magnetic imagery. Picture bulldozers with huge scoop shovels throwing dirt every which way. Men are running to keep up with the pace. There is loud noise from the machines, and black puffs of diesel smoke are present. The men shout directions back and forth, calling for more concrete, fast! Imagine yourself standing on the dirt mound. See the loose dirt piling up; smell it, feel it, even taste it if you want. Get yourself into the picture and live it as a present moment. Get it into your mind that this is happening now, not in the future. Could you use the same technique with a body disease? How about body building, or the 100-yard dash? Of course you could.

TURN WANTS INTO REALITY

By using visual imagery, it certainly seems as though you could have anything in life you wanted. After all, people under hypnotic suggestion can quickly shed their inhibitions, enabling them to exhibit extreme confidence in front of an audience, eliminate stuttering, even improve their athletic performance. Does it follow that, in a normal, conscious state, you may have anything you desire?

Let's face it. It all has to do with our true desires. If sports come more easily to you than playing the piano—and if you really like sports, you will probably find yourself out on the tennis courts much more often than sitting at the piano practicing Rachmaninoff. You may appreciate piano playing, but you love sports. See the difference?

I believe that life speaks to us through desire. The root word for desire, de-*sire*, means "of the source." If you truly listen to your desires, in any area, you can be confident that if you follow them you will be on the right track.

"That's one small step for man..."

In a recent talk to a school system, I was approached by a man who took strong issue with some of my ideas. He implied that you can't have anything you want. "I've always wanted to go to the moon," he said, "and as you can see, I don't have what I want!" I said, "You don't really want to go to the moon."

"What do you mean?" he asked. "It's been on my mind ever since I was a kid." "Sorry," I said, "I can't buy that; you don't want to go to the moon." I asked him if he had ever taken any flying lessons, any courses in aerodynamics or aircraft fight systems. Had he ever studied any meteorology, physiological functions in zero gravity, or advanced mathematics? "Well, no," he said. "Have you ever applied to the Houston Space Center for a position as an astronaut?" "No," again. "You don't want to go to the moon," I told him. "I see what you mean," he said.

I asked him what he really liked to do and he said he liked teaching kids. That is exactly what he was doing. I said to him, "I'll bet you never felt about the moon like you do about seeing kids learn."

"You're right," he said, "it gives me such a thrill when they grab on to a new idea and begin to apply it in their lives. I love it."

Yes, you can have anything you want and truly believe. You do not have to take what you get; you can get what you want and believe, but first and foremost you must be true to yourself. What is your heart's desire? Working toward anything else is misdirected effort.

14

THE SECRET TO OLYMPIAN SUCCESS

By Dennis Fox

Dennis Fox is founder of The Client Development Institute, which provides attention control training (ACT). A former top salesman for several national direct-selling organizations, he frequently speaks on the subjects of hiring, coaching, and performance improvement for corporations such as American Express, Airborne Express, Dean Witter, Hewlett Packard, National Restaurant Association and Sheraton Hotels. He also developed the "Selling The Seven C's" training courses which take a client-centered approach to selling. Phone: 800-989-SELL / 703-904-7355; e-mail: client@earthlink.net.

We've all marveled at an Olympic athlete's ability to concentrate, to focus on movement and timing and pull off a performance so perfect that it's almost magic. For me, just watching the graceful fluidity of a figure skater or the swift, controlled intensity of a perfect dive are joyous experiences in themselves. But imagine doing it! Imagine having that same centeredness, that feeling of being in control of whatever it is you are doing, no matter what's going on around you or inside your head.

The truth is, it isn't magic. Olympic athletes seem superhuman to us, and it's true that they have finely honed technical skills that they have perfected through endless hours of practice. But, many of them began as average talents who applied phenomenal persistence, large doses of determination and sheer will to achieve their outstanding performance levels.

Certainly, we do not discount the necessity of specific factors such as skill, motivation, discipline and a "believe in yourself" attitude. But, motivation, determination and attitude alone are not sufficient. Few would dispute that some level of technical talent must be innate or developed. Jack Llewellyn, sports psychologist, consultant and trainer for the Atlanta Braves, tells the story of a little league football coach who taught his players to think positively, but neglected to give them detailed instruction on how to play the game. The end result was one of his players telling the coach: "I'm *positive* I'm getting the hell kicked out of me!"

SOMETHING MORE

Let's face it; there's no doubt that high-performance achievements in athletics and sales alike are the result of a fine blend of many essential ingredients. Yet, after a 25-year career as a salesman, trainer and professional speaker, I realized that there was something beyond these well-researched and applied factors. While my students could successfully master the technical skills and rigorous practice drills of selling in the classroom they were often unable to execute the same performance, no matter how practiced, in the real world.

In an attempt to understand this phenomenon, I was led outside my discipline of Sales Performance to the realm of Olympic athletes. *What*, I wondered, enabled them to deliver consistently outstanding, finely tuned, winning performances, duplicating their trained and rehearsed performances in live competition? What was the one thing that could possibly make the difference?

The answer, and discriminator, I discovered, was *attention*, the ability not merely to "pay it," but to "play it." The capacity to call on and apply a specific type of attention to the appropriate task or challenge at hand, the ability to integrate highly developed instincts with a high degree of attention flexibility are what Olympic athletes are able to do. In *your* career, your daily life, and your relationships— the most important thing you do is—*pay attention*.

When face-to-face with any challenge, it won't matter how well-developed your skills are or how motivated you are if you're not able to pay attention. Once the critical moment is upon us and we feel the pressure to perform, how well we attend will draw the line between a highly skilled technical performance and the kind of "magic" we witness in Olympians.

YOUR ATTENTION, PLEASE!

Fortunately, thanks to the work of Robert M. Nideffer, a clinical psychologist and authority on concentration control in sports training, we have a verifiable model for helping competent sales and customer service performers and their coaches become Olympian.

Attention Control isn't simply a matter of whether or not we pay attention, it's *how* we pay attention that makes the critical difference. The challenge is to (1) give your attention to the right thing at the right time, (2) to maintain a constant balance, and (3) be able to shift from one kind of attention to another, with the graceful fluidity of an Olympic skater, as the situation demands.

As Dr. Nideffer determined, there are four possible ways of paying attention. He created a formalized model and a tool to measure our attentional strengths and liabilities: The Attentional and Interpersonal Style Inventory (TAIS) as well as a language that enables us to clearly define attention style so that we can assess, predict, and control the way we pay attention. While each of us has natural tendencies toward one or two attentional modes, it has been proven that we can learn to achieve an important balance of all four types of attention and access the right one at exactly the right moment.

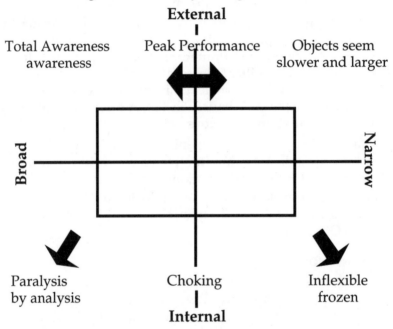

From *Psyched to Win*, Robert M. Nideffer, Ph.D. (Leisure Press: Champaign, Ill., 1992). Reprinted with permission from the publisher.

The chart illustrates the dimensions of consciousness, or what we might call the field of attention. Your attention has a direction and a focus; direction is either internal or external and focus is either broad or narrow. The square in the center is the normal experience of consciousness, in which you shift around the field, but never too extremely in any one direction. Outside the box are the areas in which you can become immersed and, as the illustration shows, internal immersion can result in paralysis. It is in the external, in "the zone," that our peak performances await us. When our internal attention becomes automatic, we can attend to the external world and achieve unlimited awareness.

EXAMPLES ON THE GREEN

To get an idea of what I mean by the right kind of attention, picture a golf tournament. Jack Nicklaus has been considered one of the greatest golfers of all time. Picture Jack as he is preparing to sink a difficult putt. There's a big crowd gathered around the green. Without being able to block out the crowd, Jack couldn't give his full attention to the technical details: the lay of the ball, the slope of the surface, the texture of the green, the angle of the putter, and so forth.

Also on the scene is a security guard. To do his job, although very tempting, he cannot pay too much attention to Jack's upcoming phenomenal performance. His attention must be given to broadly sweeping the crowd to pick up any unusual movements.

In this example, Jack Nicklaus and the security guard at the golf tournament demonstrate how specific types of attention are needed for certain tasks. Jack Nicklaus needed a "broad external" focus of attention to assess the conditions of the green and then, when he was ready to make his stroke, he had to shift to "narrow internal," to check his grip and maintain perfect control and coordination of his body. If he had again shifted to "broad external"—perhaps distracted by the crowd—he likely would have lost his concentration, and his "narrow internal" attention might have recognized disturbing inner thoughts or self-consciousness. But Jack learned long ago to reduce and control that tendency. He understood that a distraction is really nothing more than an *attraction* to the wrong thing.

Suppose the security guard, who has a natural tendency toward a "broad external" attentional style, apprehends a perpetrator at the tournament. When called upon to testify in court, due to his "broad external" tendency, the security guard becomes so distracted by the courtroom environment that his testimony is weak and unconvincing. Ultimately, the perpetrator gets away.

PLATEAU BREAKER

In training situations, I often encounter sales people who have reached a plateau, a place where they feel "stuck." They know their product, have great skills, make lots of contacts, and often book a full schedule of appointments. Even after passing these "tests," when they get in front of the client and the pressure for performance is still on, they falter on the appropriate use of the right attentional style that will determine their very success.

Let me illustrate the concepts in the context of a sales person in the course of some common activities. As he begins his day, his thoughts are focused on developing a game plan for an afternoon sales call. To prepare, he attempts to anticipate the client's concerns as well as a strong strategy of response and action. At this point, the sales person must use a "broad internal " mode of attention.

In the car on the way to the appointment, he conducts the mental rehearsal of this plan by shifting to a "narrow internal" mode. When he arrives at the call, he is surprised to find there are two additional people in the meeting. One of two scenarios can now follow.

Scenario One: The sales person is unnerved by the unexpected participants. His pulse begins to race, his heart is pounding in his head. The fright or flight instinct causes him to choke. Remembering a similar predicament that had a poor outcome, he is overwhelmed by narrow internal attentional focus. He becomes paralyzed and uses only narrow external attention to focus on the scheduled client, missing important cues from the other participants, who turn out to be key players in the decision-making process.

For what is true physically, applies mentally; you can't be in two places at one time. By focusing internally on his own thoughts, he missed the important cues that could have made this a winning performance.

Now, scenario two: Quick on his mental feet, the sales person rapidly integrates the two additional people in the meeting and calls on the power of Attention Control Training. By applying Olympic training techniques, like "centering," using diaphragmatic breathing and the mental integration of specially chosen "trigger" words, the trained sales person responds to the "surprise" participants by shifting to a broad external mode. He assesses the nonverbal cues of the people in the room, and then quickly shifts to broad internal to interpret the role and impact these players will have in the buying decision before moving to a quick narrow internal period that allows him to regroup. Quickly, he shifts again to the narrow external mode for a focused, successful presentation.

What made *the* difference in these two scenarios? It wasn't technical skill, motivation or attitude. It was the level of *attentional* skill, and the ability to recover quickly and shift back and forth between attention styles as the need dictated. This is how good performers become great. It's how great performers, who have seemingly plateaued, can move forward.

ATTENTION DEFICIT

As an adult with an attention deficit disorder, I spent many years succeeding by compensating for my lack of attention control through sheer guts and determination, having peak experiences and calling it "luck." It wasn't until I saw my own young son suffer and struggle with his inherited disorder that I gained a real appreciation for the critically important role of the ability to pay attention in the right way at the right time.

This personal experience allowed me to understand my own attentional deficits and make the appropriate corrections; attentional corrections that have allowed me to improve my own performance and those of the Olympic sales professionals I coach each year.

In whatever work you do, you too can learn to strike a perfect balance of all four attention styles and use what you need when you need it. You can reach a point where the four types of attention-paying are so integrated within you that the shifts from one to another are as fluid and graceful as a figure skater. This kind of attentional integration will heighten your experience so that peak performance comes almost naturally.

An accomplished diver, Robert Nideffer describes his recollection of a perfect dive:

> I was warming up and made the decision to perform a reverse dive with one half-twist in a layout position…It's a pretty dive alright, but it can be frightening because the first part of it is blind, that is, you can't see the board or the water. On this particular occasion I came up off the board in perfect position.

It was as though something had clicked inside of me. I knew exactly where my body was relative to the board even though I couldn't see it. I had perfect control over my body and crystal-clear, complete awareness of what was going on. Time seemed slowed down as if everything were happening in slow motion. I floated up, up, up. As I reached the very top of the dive, I seemed to hang in the air. I knew that a good portion of my body was over the board and I knew that I would miss hitting the board by about three inches. As I began to drop a shoulder and twist I heard the screams of the crowd. They thought I was going to hit the board. As I was twisting, my eyes went past the people and I saw very clearly the expressions on their faces and the fear in their eyes. I instinctively smiled, feeling such power and control. I exalted in knowing exactly where I was and in thrilling the crowd. I turned my body and dropped three inches from the board to complete what had to be one of the most perfect dives of my life (*Psyched to Win*).

Notice how integrated his experience is and how many levels of attention he is able to balance (*balance* is the key word here). It's amazing that, even under the pressure of this performance, in a dive that probably lasted three seconds, he was able to focus momentarily on the faces in the crowd and register their expressions and even the look in their eyes. What awareness! It's equally amazing that he is able to recall almost every second with perfect clarity and share it with us, right down to his internal sense of power, his instinctive smile, and his recollection of time seeming to slow down.

Let's look specifically at how the diver gave all levels of attention to his spectacular dive:

Broad external—hearing the screams of the crowd, registering their fear (broad internal) that he would hit the board;

Narrow internal—all the motions of his body in synchronization and in proper relationship to the board;

Broad external—the expressions on the faces of the people and the fear (broad internal) in their eyes;

Narrow external—his own exalted feeling of power and control, his smile.

Notice also how one level of attention accentuates and reinforces another. If he hadn't heard the screams of the crowd and seen the looks on their faces, the diver would not have experienced the more subtle sense of thrilling them. Because he was sensitive to their realization that he might hit the board, his feeling of being in control was heightened and his achievement was much more momentous.

The slowing of time that the diver experienced is one sure indicator that natural attentional shifts were propelling him to the heights of his potential.

After this process becomes so natural that you don't have to attend to it, you will find that you are able to block out task-irrelevant cues, even if you are a "broad external" type. You will be able to avoid becoming too immersed in any one area to "choke" your performance. Once you are reading your environment and making automatic shifts in attention, you'll be functioning at the level we call "unconscious competence."

Emerson Fittipaldi, a former Grand Prix champion, describes how a driver operates through four channels that are incredibly reminiscent of the attentional modes discussed in this chapter. All at once, this peak performer is pays attention to what his body is doing, looks ahead to anticipate turns, checks to see who's to his left and to his right, and finally, evaluates the condition of his car and determines when to make a pit stop. When you drive your own car, some of these things are in the background while your attention is focused on what you feel is most important. You tune out the sound of the engine until it sounds unusual and causes concern.

It is simple—but not always so easy. To get started, pick an area in which you are highly motivated. It may be your golf game, listening more effectively to your children, or making speeches. When you have improved your attention-paying in an area that is important to you, and you can see the difference it makes, you will be able to apply it to many more areas of your life and eventually integrate attentional balancing into your total being.

Here are the steps:

1. *Define the attentional demands of the job you want to do.* Recognize that it may require more than one, and that certain aspects of the task will require certain types of attentional skills.

2. *Break these down for yourself* and see how you think you'll do and where you'll need to improve.

3. *Ask yourself what personality traits you have that might intensify your attentional style.* If you have high social needs and like to have regular approval and input, a job in scientific research will probably drive you to distraction, but you might make a great salesperson.

4. *Recognize your strengths and your weaknesses,* and above all else, respect them. Put yourself in positions where you can utilize your strengths.

5. *Delegate what you cannot do well,* and team up with other people to enhance and expand your abilities and work off of theirs.

15

WORLD-CLASS TEAMWORK & THE CHALLENGE OF WORKING WITH DIFFICULT PEOPLE

Gerry Faust, Ph. D.,   and   Clark Wigley

Gerry Faust is an entrepreneur, behavioral scientist, academician and consultant to a broad range of business, professional and government organizations. He is currently president of Faust Management Corporation in San Diego, an international consulting firm providing executive coaching, training and development, strategic planning and organizational redesign. Dr. Faust is the originator and co-creator of Executive Insight ®, a guided process of discovery, decision making, and action planning. Phone: 800-835-0533 / 619-536-7970; e-mail: faustmgmt@aol. com.

Clark Wigley has 20 years of experience in management, marketing, product development and sales. He is currently CEO of LOIS, Inc., a rapidly growing legal information electronic publisher and a founding partner of the Regulatory Resource Center, an Internet-based administrative law publisher. In addition to his operating experience, Wigley spent eight years as a strategic management consultant where he completed assignments in data processing, publishing, transportation, health care, banking and real estate for clients such as IBM, American Airlines and the Bank of America.

As much as we'd sometimes like to be, no man is an island, especially in the world of modern organizations. The tasks we have to accomplish, the levels of service and productivity we have to deliver, and a variety of other challenges, make it imperative that responsible workers, managers and leaders also be responsible team members and team leaders.

The words *complementary* and *interdisciplinary* are often used to describe these teams because they generally bring together people with different backgrounds and skills or people from different parts of the organizations. For those of us who find ourselves on these teams, however, we know that the word "complementary" may apply to how the team looks on paper, but it is not always an accurate description of how the team really works. Personality problems often come to the surface on these kinds of teams. The presence of this situation is revealed through subtle comments heard in the halls or around the coffee machine that go something like this:

"Can you believe what that guy just said? Is it just me or is that guy Ralph the biggest jerk you have ever seen?"

It seems that no matter what we do, there are always one or two of these "Ralphs" on our teams. You know who they are: They are clever devils whose hard work or brilliant insights are matched only by their amazing ability to be unbelievably aggravating to work with. The obvious solution is to get rid of the "Ralphs." It is our experience that this tactic should be the last solution to be pursued for several reasons. First, Ralph may sometimes be the boss, so getting rid of him (or her) is not an option. Second, and more important, the team was put together for a specific reason and Ralph may have a specialized expertise that is vital to the success of the team. By the way, through some inexplicable law of the universe, it is often true that the more critical the contribution, the bigger the jerk. Finally, business periodicals are full of examples where Ralph left the organization to go on and build a wildly successful new company, pursuing the identical work he got fired for. Thus, the success of the project, the team, the department, or even the entire organization can depend upon our collective ability to draw practical and useful the contributions from these difficult people.

FOUR ROLES OF MANAGEMENT

Before we can begin to work with Ralph, it is helpful to understand what causes people to be difficult in the first place. Theories of personality and work style have been studied for centuries.

The basics of the model used here were first published in *How to Solve the Mismanagement Crisis* (1979) by Dr. Ichak Adizes. These provide an excellent foundation for understanding work style by focusing first on what is important in making organizations work. After studying literally hundreds of organizations and managers around the world during a 20-year period, Dr. Adizes proposed that to be successful over time, an organization, whether it be a team, a department, a company or an entire country, must balance four basic roles. He further proposed that if an organization balances these roles, they provide both necessary and sufficient conditions for success. That is, if all four roles are kept in balance, the organization will be optimally managed and will be successful (profitable) over both the short- and long-term. Here is a brief description of Adizes' four roles of management.

The first and foremost role of an organization is to Produce Results (P). All organizations were designed for a purpose. That purpose centers around producing certain results. This role causes the organization to focus on *what* it is supposed to be doing and constantly pressures for continuous progress towards this goal. When well executed, this role ensures that the organization will be effective over the short term.

It is, however, not enough just to produce results. To be successful, organizations need to produce results efficiently and consistently. The Administering (A) role is the second critical role. This role has to do with getting things organized and systematized. This role focuses on *how* things are being done. In this way the organization is pressured to optimize the use of its limited resources. This ensures the efficiency and consistency of the organization over the short term. Organizations and people who are good at this role have two basic qualities: logical, systematic thinking and meticulous, close attention to detail.

The world constantly changes. So do the needs of customers, the technologies we use, the competitors we face and the environments in which we operate. To keep ahead of these changes, an organization must also be constantly changing and adapting. Entrepreneuring is the third critical role of any organization. To Entrepreneur (E) is to change the organization to best meet the future. This role focuses the organization on looking forward, proactively adapting to future needs, opportunities and threats to ensure its long-term viability. Successful Entrepreneuring requires creativity and the willingness to take risks.

The fourth critical role of management focuses on developing teamwork, synergy and an overall sense of mission in the organization. This role of Integrating (I) an organization allows a group of individuals to become an organization, a company, a team. It also reduces the dependency of the organization on specific individuals. Organizations and people who are good at this role develop a sense of mutual interest and mutual trust. To be good at this role people must be sensitive to the needs of others and good listeners, facilitators, and communicators.

If an organization (team, department, company, etc.) is successful at balancing these four roles then it will be successful over time. The first two roles focus on what to do and how to do it in the short term. They ensure short-term effectiveness and efficiency. The second two roles focus us on what to do and how to manage over the long term. If any of these roles is missing or underplayed, the organization will be predictably mismanaged.

WORK STYLES

The Adizes model of management roles has an analogue in the area of personality or work style. Just as you can describe organizations in terms of Producing, Administering, Entrepreneuring, and Integrating, so can you also describe people. As individuals we generally have some capability to fill each of these roles, but people have a tendency to be more capable in, or to emphasize, one or two of these four roles more than the others. Our work style colors how we interact with our colleagues, customers and our work place. People with different work styles notice different things, think different things are important, respond differently and communicate differently. In fact, most of us find people with different work styles difficult to deal with. Remember Ralph? Ralph probably has a work style that's different from yours. Since work styles transcend sex roles, consider the following as archetypal character studies of work styles.

THE PRODUCER

The Producer is driven. The Producer wants to succeed, to achieve and be admired for his efforts. His work is his source of pride. He arrives early, leaves late, and works like crazy in between. Even though he may leave the office late, look what he takes with him—his briefcase! He just wants to keep that work close, just in case he "needs it." By the way, he will carry that brief case back and forth, even though he doesn't get around to opening it evening after evening after evening. The Producer's work space is often a mess. There is work everywhere. If you ask him, "How is it going?" (and you're going to have a hard time getting him to stop long enough to answer the question), he will answer with an extended discourse on how busy he is and how much he has done. When he tells you that he arrived at 6 a.m. and won't be able to leave until 9 p.m. and is leaving the next day on a business trip to Buffalo, is he complaining? No, not really. He's bragging. He is pointing out how he lives up to the "hard work" standard he has set.

Producers have a hard time delegating. Remember, delegating is giving away something they love and "need"—work! When they get frustrated with others they often "take the work away" from them. This will happen even if the offender works for them or if they have just "delegated" that work. Often it appears that they find it more difficult to explain how to do a job than to do it themselves. If you come to Producers with a problem, don't expect advice, expect them to take over the task. And, they will take on the task even though you know and they know they are already overcommitted.

THE ADMINISTRATOR

The Administrator seeks order and consistency. He likes to manage "by the book" and he likes things neat and organized. When asked to make decisions he is careful in his analysis, considers all the data and certainly doesn't want to make any errors. (The Entrepreneur, in contrast, will accept mistakes to ensure she takes advantage of all opportunities.) The Administrator may miss opportunities in order to prevent mistakes. It has been said that Administrators "would rather be precisely wrong than approximately correct."

Being on time is often a commitment, a way of life, for the Administrator. He arrives at work on time, generally not early and certainly not late. He also leaves on time. Even if the office is in a crisis, he will leave because it's 5:00 p.m. He has to leave then because he has other things scheduled…and, of course, he must adhere to his schedule. He keeps his desk neat…inside and out. Things are often arranged in the proper place on that desk every night before the Administrator leaves. If you want an interesting experience, look inside a desk drawer. Often you can't because it's locked. But if you could, you would find the paper clips sorted in compartments by size and the rubber bands neatly bound together. If there are different colored rubber bands, they are generally in separate bundles. The most compelling detail, however, are the pencils—always sharp! The process that keeps them that way must be fascinating to watch.

Administrators will delegate clearly with lots of detail. They follow through and follow through and follow through. If there is a policy, they stick to it and, in fact, regularly add to the policy manual based on one-time events that indicate the organization is "out of control."

THE ENTREPRENEUR

The Entrepreneur is a creative risk taker. She is not always (or even often) constrained by the limitations of reality. Much of what is important to her goes on in the mind. Entrepreneurs strongly believe the dictum, "What can be thought can be achieved," although the Entrepreneur may not know how. The Entrepreneur looks at what is and thinks about what could be. She certainly doesn't let data stand in the way of great thoughts, theories or even plans. She does not like details, or things or people who interfere with or throw cold water on great thoughts.

Entrepreneurs appear to march to the beat of their own drummers. When does she come to work? Who knows? When does she follow up? Who knows? When does she call with an assignment or to share a brilliant insight? Who knows? The meetings of Entrepreneurs are spontaneous. "Everyone into the conference room; it's time for a meeting." And, her meetings are exciting! They keep you on the edge of your seat. In fact, you may not even get completely "sat" before the "big E" starts talking. She talks during meetings. She often thinks while, rather than before, she speaks. She then measures the success of a meeting by the number of new ideas she gets. People who attend her meetings may have an exciting time but often wonder what was decided or what it was all about. A colleague was once heard to say after one Entrepreneur's meeting, "I think we were just supposed to experience it!"

The Entrepreneur uses ideas to shake up the organization. She thinks outside of the box and is seldom constrained by what is. Entrepreneurs generally drive Administrators crazy!

THE INTEGRATOR

The Integrator constantly tries to improve communication, facilitate meetings, encourage participation, create consensus and build the team. He is generally emphatic, communicative, a good listener, supportive and nurturing. He is constantly gathering input, and doing environmental impact studies (How did that impact the people in the typing pool?). He likes coming to work when everyone else does. He keeps his door open and wants his desk where people can easily drop by. He is prepared to listen for a long time to almost anything. He likes meetings and group process. He listens at meetings while everyone else talks. He may seem wishy-washy in his decision-making because he wants to be supportive of the ideas of others and likes to stay flexible and keep his options open. The Integrator likes to make decisions in a team environment. Integrators drive Producers crazy!

A person's work style is easily recognized. It allows you to predict how he or she will react in specific situations and can help you decide how to manage, motivate, communicate with or sell to him or her. You can get clues to someone's work style the first time you meet, and often before the conversation begins.

Look around the office. The Producer decorates his office with work and symbols of achievement. The desk is messy and the shelves and walls hold trophies, awards and certificates. The sign on the wall is likely to say, "Lead, follow or get out of the way!" The Administrator's office is neat and basic. There may be a few charts and graphs, a company handbook and a diploma or two. The Entrepreneur surrounds herself with abstract art, books or hundreds on hundreds of topics (mostly unread), witty sayings and weird contraptions. The Integrator prefers pictures of friends and the team from past company picnics or strategic planning sessions.

You can also tell differences in style when you talk to people. If you ask a Producer what time it is, what does he do? He glances at his watch and growls, "9:50," accompanied by a look that says, "and how dare you interrupt me from what is clearly a very important task." How about the Administrator? He will study his watch and say "9:53 and a half," reflecting his desire to be very precise. If you ask an Integrator what time it is, he'll say, "9:53, why are you asking?" And before you know it, you are immersed in an extended conversation. If you ask the Entrepreneur, you can get two answers. A common response is that she doesn't know because she doesn't wear a watch. The other is, "Oh, about 10:00." Even if she did have a watch she might not be able to tell the time very accurately because the watch is likely one of those trendy things that has no numbers on it. Entrepreneurs have a unique relationship with time that is very different from the other styles. You may want to remember this when you are working with "jerks" who habitually show up late to meetings. Why do Entrepreneurs often show up late to a meeting? Because they don't measure time by an external standard. They don't have a watch on their arms because their clocks are internal. To an Entrepreneur, it is time when it is time. This is what allows them to show up 20 minutes late for a meeting and say, "Okay I'm here, let's get going" and then be absolutely shocked when all the Producers, Administrators and Integrators who got there on time, go nuts.

By the way, it is true that under different situations, each of us may "flex" and temporarily modify our work styles. But it is also true that over time most of us will exhibit behavior that is generally consistent with our dominant work style. It is not as important to know exactly what style a person is, as it is to recognize that you have a style and they have a style and to understand the differences between your two styles.

So, who's the jerk?

Let's take a minute and look back at the "Ralph is a jerk" comment. Which of these styles is the style of a "jerk?" Take a moment and write down some words that come to your mind to describe each of the four styles. For example, Producers might be described as go-getters or doers. Really aggressive Producers might also be described as pushy, hard-charging or maybe even domineering. Do a similar exercise for each of the other styles. Every style can be described with words that have positive or negative connotations. The negatively loaded words are ones we might use to describe the jerk. Thus, the only logical conclusion is that either all of us are jerks or none of us are jerks. Whether someone is a "jerk" or not depends mostly on who is doing the evaluating and how Ralph's style contrasts with the person doing the evaluating.

Working with ralph

Labeling someone as a "jerk" is actually not a problem. The problem is all the decisions that get made after that label is attached. These subsequent decisions usually go something like this, "I've tried to work with the guy, but he's a lost cause. I can't work, I won't work with the guy. I want him off my team." Often the relationship is so damaged that the two parties involved never can work together again in any meaningful and productive way. However, we have seldom seen situations where the contributions of two jerks could not be integrated and made productive. Working with difficult people is just like making good spaghetti sauce. If you have the right ingredients, good equipment and follow the recipe, you can turn out a pretty tasty product. You have the ingredients (the work styles), you have the equipment (brain, ears and mouth), now all you need is a recipe that is easy to follow. The recipe for success when working with difficult people has these three steps:

- Alter your feelings about conflict.
- Recognize the need for each style's unique contribution.
- Know how to speak the language of other work styles.

Remember, you don't have to like all your coworkers, you just have to be able to work with them.

ALTER YOUR FEELING ABOUT CONFLICT

Recognizing and dealing with differences in style is at the heart of working with difficult people. As we have said, generally people you find difficult are people who have a different work style from yours. Different styles have different filters which "color" everything they see, feel, and hear. For example, if all four of our examples of working styles walked up to a window that looked out onto New York City, what would they see? The Producer, who focuses on the immediate task, might take a quick look at the city, and say something like, "New York, what's the big deal?" and then sit back down and start reading his mail or thinking about all the "real work" he has back on his desk. The Administrator, on the other hand, would likely see a dirty window and wonder who is in charge of maintenance and how much is charged for this shoddy work. The Entrepreneur, who sees the bigger picture, would say, "New York, the Big Apple, Land of Opportunity!" and probably start thinking about some farfetched scheme to start a new business. Lastly, the Integrator, who is the shepherd of the organization, may not even look out the window at all. He would see a group of people standing at the window, apparently having a pretty good time, and would focus his energy on making sure that everyone has a good view.

Given these different perspectives, what do you think will happen when we assemble these four styles together to decide what we should do about New York? Do you think that "personality" problems will start to show up? The Entrepreneur will stand up and say, "I've got a great idea…" The Administrator will follow with, "Let me tell you why that is the dumbest idea you have had all day," and the contest begins. After 15 minutes of screaming and shouting, the Producer will interrupt, look at his watch as say, "Hold it, we've already been here for 15 minutes and nothing is happening. If you guys can't make up your minds, I'm leaving," which sets off the Integrator who pleads, "Look guys, every time we get together, we always end up fighting. Why can't we work better together?"

Whenever we get a team of different styles together this kind of scuffling will occur. Is this conflict bad? Most of us have negative reactions to conflict and will go to great lengths to avoid it. *This avoidance can be a big mistake!* In our desire to avoid conflict, we may eliminate conflicting points of view, points of view we can learn from. This is a proven recipe for disaster. We must recognize that a lot of the conflict we experience is conflict of style and not conflict of ideas. We must learn to look past the style conflict and get on with the real discussion. If we *don't* generate conflict, we have a problem. It is from interacting with people with different perspectives that we learn, expand our own perspectives, and fashion new and creative solutions. Conflict is desirable. Conflict is like nuclear energy. We have to be careful with it because it can be used to light up or blow up your team, but its presence is absolutely essential. We must not eliminate conflict. We must create it and then learn how to use its energy productively.

RECOGNIZE EACH STYLE'S UNIQUE CONTRIBUTION

Going back to our New York window, the next question to ask is, "So which perspective is right?" Remember for any organization (team, department or company) to be successful over the long term, it must balance the four roles of management. In a related way, key decisions should be made based on a balance of the different perspectives provided by different styles. Thus, the answer to the question is, "All are right," and all perspectives are needed to create the total picture.

Each style incorporate both strengths and weaknesses. The Producer may force us to focus on results, keep us on track and not let us forget why we're in the meeting. At the same time, he may not see the long-term problems created by quickly defined solutions or be able to design the announcement so others will accept the decision.

It's all right to see and even laugh at the idiosyncrasies of someone else's style as long as we recognize that we each have our own styles that also offer lots of opportunities for laughter. But, it is even more important that we admit our weaknesses and search for the strengths in others.

KNOW HOW TO SPEAK THEIR LANGUAGE

If you want to communicate with, work with, motivate or manage people, you have to learn to speak their languages. And different styles speak different languages. Many believe that the way to work with people well is to follow the Golden Rule: "Do unto others as you would have them do unto you."

In other words, treat other people the same way that you want them to treat you. This is great advice for dealing with many aspects of our lives, but it is precisely what gets us into trouble when dealing with different work styles. If you are a Producer, applying the Golden Rule would mean treating all your teammates as fellow Producers. Only other Producers like to be treated in this manner. Producers like to move quickly, are action oriented, want decisions now and don't like to "over analyze things." Administrators want all the facts before they decide, they don't want to be wrong and they want to carefully plan the follow-through on decisions. The fact that Producers communicate in "P" (the language of Producers) and want to make decisions in that style is what causes Administrators (who speak "A" and like to decide things in an "A" way) to think that Producers are "jerks." Working with different styles requires the application of a different rule, one that Tony Alessandra has called the Platinum Rule: "Do unto others as they would have themselves done unto."

If you are a Producer, you have to learn how to talk like an Administrator, an Entrepreneur or an Integrator, if you want to work well with these different styles. What is their language? For example, Producers and Entrepreneurs tend to think, speak and decide rapidly, Administrators and Integrators prefer to think, speak and decide much more slowly.

You might ask: "Does this mean Producers and Entrepreneurs are smarter, have greater insight?" Not really. It's just a style difference. Producers want to get to the result. They want to act, so they jump to conclusions. It is also the case that for Producers, the world has less "gray:" it's more black and white. The question they ask is, "Does this get me to my goal?" If the answer is "yes"—they act. Why have further discussions? Notice that Producers might ignore long-term consequences, the effects on others, and many other things because of their "bias for action." Entrepreneurs decide quickly because they don't "sweat the details." They think intuitively and often decide based on their gut reactions. Notice that both Administrators and Integrators may prefer a slower pace and may decide more slowly. But also notice they do so for different reasons. Administrators decide more slowly because they want all the data. Integrators decide more slowly because they want more input from others and will take the time to achieve consensus.

Each style brings a benefit. The Producer's bias for action moves things along; the Administrator's search for data keeps us from making errors. Yet these strengths themselves are often the point of conflict.

If you want to motivate, manage, sell to or communicate with a Producer: Get to the point, focus on the near-term result, let him know what the goal is. If you are dealing with an Administrator: Slow down, present the facts, give him time to ask questions and consider the data, walk him through a logical process. The next time you're dealing with a difficult person, consider: What's his or her style? What is my style? How do I have to present things so he will feel comfortable? How can I speak her language? Even in a meeting you can help facilitate understanding and avoid destructive conflict by rephrasing one language into another, or by reminding others of the style needs of their colleagues. Here are some helpful words heard in recent meetings. "I don't think Bob wants to rush me so much that we make a poor decision, but he is right—we can't discuss this all day." "What Grace is trying to say is that the answer may not be as simple as we think. Maybe we should slow down and consider it from a couple of other angles."

BACK-UP BEHAVIOR

One of the major reasons that an understanding of style is so critical to building world-class teams is that style conflicts can be the key factor in driving people into back-up behavior. Back-up behavior is the flip side of a working style's productive behavior. It's the reaction to excessive pressure from an organization's culture, the climate of a situation or the different style of a teammate. People like being in cultures and climates which are consistent with their styles and they like dealing with people who are "comfortable." Comfortable is another way of saying "with the same style as mine." When our environment or the tenor of a discussion moves away from our style, we become less comfortable; and if the move is too great, or too long, the reaction is a shift to back-up behavior.

Back-up behavior for each style is dysfunctional and predictable. Each style has its own characteristic back-up behavior. The back-up style for Administrators and Integrators is passive. Administrators withdraw, Integrators submit. In the Entrepreneur-dominated meeting with its characteristic flights of fancy, visions of the future and suspension of reality, the Administrator can get overwhelmed, and frustrated. The reaction is often to take out other work, decide it's time to go to the restroom, get a cup of coffee. He is withdrawing. The Administrator will send a signal that he is withdrawing. He will fold his arms, become quiet and get a glassy look in his eyes. Physically, he is still present, but mentally, he has left. When he has had enough, he may invoke a rule: "Well, it's time to go home, I'm out of here. You said this meeting was going to be over at 4:30, it's 4:35 and I'm already late to another meeting." Even if he doesn't have another meeting, he is up and out of the room. By the way, he also remembers. The Administrator takes notes, has a memory like an elephant, and often retaliates in his own way.

The Integrator is generally impacted greatly by a Producer's behavior. In the face of all that energy and drive, the Integrator may cave in: "Whatever you guys want is OK with me," he says. But, that's not really what he means. Rather, he is sending his signal, hoping that some caring person will see it and stop what's going on and give him another chance to present his case. If not, he is prepared to lie in the road and get run over by the tank commander (P) and his crew.

Producers and Entrepreneurs are not passive in their back-up behaviors. Don't worry, you will notice it! Producers dictate,

Entrepreneurs attack. You can already guess what sets these people off. For the Producer, it's moving too slowly, too much concern about the "fuzzy things" (you know, people, feelings, etc.) or an unwillingness to act. When he has had enough, the Producer takes over. He says, "I'll take care of it myself." Or, in a meeting, if he is in charge, he stands up and says, "Here's what we're going to do, No. 1, No. 2, No. 3," and then as he walks out, almost as an afterthought, he says, "Thanks for your input, meeting's over." As you sit there in stunned silence, wondering what just hit you, it's easy to say, "What a jerk!"

Entrepreneurs are driven to distraction by an interruption of their stream of consciousness, too much attention to detail and phrases like, "That won't work" or "Yes, but...." When the Entrepreneur has had enough, she generally attacks and often humiliates those who are holding her back. She, too, sends a signal: rolling eyes, long exhales, and hands over the eyes are pretty common. These Vesuvian signals are indications that the Entrepreneur is about to blow. If the signals don't get an immediate reaction, the attack begins. It may start with ingratiating comments like, "Let me explain this to you...one...more...time." It proceeds through a well-articulated presentation of the importance of the ideas and the conceptual context of the situation. It is often interrupted as the Entrepreneur becomes frustrated by having to do all this explaining and her conclusion often includes a statement like, "I often wonder if you're really up to this level of thinking," or some similar ego-deflating remark. The other styles' response to the attack is generally not uttered aloud but is often internally contemplated, "Boy what a jerk."

The point of all this is that back-up behavior is the downfall of teams. It is unproductive and even destructive. It does not reflect the best of a style, it reflects the worst. It does not allow people to make their much needed contributions or provide their complementary views. When you recognize back-up behavior, you ought to stop the activity, get everyone to take a deep breath (or call a break) and then try to refocus on where you are, what you're trying to accomplish and what you need to do from that point.

Even more important, try to head off back-up behavior at the pass. Don't let it emerge. Learn to create climates that are tolerable for the whole team, discuss some guidelines for your meeting behavior, discuss what can be done to make meetings more successful, and help everyone learn to speak the language of their colleagues.

Functionalizing the contributions of "jerks" is a difficult and long-term pursuit. But it is critical to helping you create and maintain world-class teams.

16

THE GAMES APPLIED TO REAL LIFE: THE INSIGHTS OF TWO OLYMPIANS

Dennis McCuistion, C.S.P. and Niki McCuistion, C.S.P.

Dennis McCuistion was a bank CEO at age 29 and Niki McCuistion was in sales and sales management. They have co-authored four books and hundreds of articles on business and banking success strategies. Niki produces and Dennis hosts the nationally syndicated, issue-oriented "McCuistion" television show broadcast on PBS. Their public speaking programs are researched and tailored to meet their clients' strategic needs in leadership, quality service, change management, peak performance, finance and communication Phone: 800-543-0310 / 972-255-2599; e-mail: mccuisti@ix.netcom.com; web site: mccuistiontv.com.

W hat is the magic of the Olympics? Why does an event that takes place every four years have us saluting and revering the athletes who go the extra mile? Is it that we hunger for what the Olympics represent? Do they satisfy a central need within us for sharing moments of achievement? The Olympic principles of striving for excellence, fair play and ethics strike a resonating chord in each of us.

Every two years the world celebrates the glory of achievement as we witness the very best from the athletes who compete in the Olympic Games. They are the best in the world. The athletes from each country represent the finest in all of us, or at least we want them to.

The magnitude of the Olympics is awe-inspiring. There is no more magnificent event anywhere. It is an event that is watched on television by 2.5 billion people around the world. Each Olympic event dazzles us with what the human spirit and the human body can accomplish. The spirit embodied in the Olympics can be modeled as everyday guiding principles as well. It brings out the best performances in us daily, on the job and at home, just as it does in the athletes we salute.

OLYMPIC BEGINNINGS

The basic difference between the original Greek Olympic games and the modern games is that the Greeks were saluting their gods. Today, we salute our heroes. We still honor the values of the Olympic movement started in ancient times: the striving for excellence in mind, body and spirit. The original Olympics brought together the best in competition and promoted collaboration among the nations participating. (In ancient times, all wars would cease during the Olympic games. The modern games were cancelled in 1916, 1940 and 1944 because of war.) Eventually, "professionalism" was fostered, and as humans were glorified, the original purpose of the Olympics (to honor and glorify the gods) was put aside. The games were officially ended in 394 A.D. when it was felt they had too many pagan connotations.

Baron Pierre de Coubertin, a young French nobleman, is responsible for the revival of the Olympics in 1896. He believed he could restore the ancient Greek ideal of the balanced development of mind and body and succeeded in restoring both the games and the ideals associated with them. Even though the games have been politicized to some degree, they still embody the best of us all. The idea of the world's best athletes coming together to compete in a peaceful arena, and promoting the Olympic ideals, unifies countries during those electric moments when the games are played. Certainly, from the athletes' point of view, the goals have been at least partially realized.

Are there glitches? The inevitable use of the Olympics as a weapon of war and terrorism has taken its toll. They've been used and abused by the Nazis, boycotted by various countries—including ours—to protest seizure of countries by perceived aggressors. Unfortunately, political overtones crept in during 1956 when Egypt, Iraq and Lebanon boycotted the Melbourne games to protest the Anglo–French seizure of the Suez canal, and the Netherlands, Spain and Switzerland boycotted to protest the U.S.S.R.'s invasion of Hungary. In 1968, Americans John Carlos and Tommy Smith used the Mexico City games to protest U.S. racial discrimination. The tragic massacre of eleven Israeli athletes in 1972 by Palestinian terrorists brought the Munich games to its knees. In 1976 at the Montreal games, 33 African nations (which would have had 400 athletes participating) boycotted to protest South Africa's apartheid practices.

In 1980 the Untied States boycotted the games in Moscow to protest the Soviet invasion of Afghanistan. Forty nations followed the United State's lead and it put a decided damper on the games as it eliminated the Soviet's chief athletic competition. The fears of many that the future of the Olympic movement was in jeopardy were well founded. In 1984 at the Los Angeles summer games, the Soviet Union lead an Eastern bloc boycott. In spite of the political reasons for nations boycotting, the games have survived.

SUCCESS JUNKIES

Yet, while the Olympic movement has survived the political machinations of nations, can it survive the destructive side of the very spirit it represents, glorifies, and that rivets us to our TV sets?

How can we glorify our athletes when they—our heroes/gods we exalt today—abuse the principles of the Olympic movement? In 1988 Canadian Ben Johnson was disqualified for using performance enhancing substances in his urge to win at any cost.

The Olympic movement should—and does—provide the ultimate opportunity for fair play. The goal includes the struggle as well as the achievement. Yet in our world today we are rewarded more and more only for winning. Our society is focused on success. Unfortunately, success at all costs sullies the journey. It is a habit of our society to think short term: hurry up and make it; instant gratification; accumulate medals and accolades. Many want the pot of gold at the end of the rainbow, thinking the only purpose of the rainbow is the pot of gold, not the rainbow itself.

It is easy to see how we can be confused, because we only remember the winners. The more gold an athlete gets, the more successful we regard him or her. We remember winners such as Florence Griffith Joyner, Eric Heiden and Bill Johnson (the first American man to win an Olympic alpine ski title). We remember Wilma Rudolph, who conquered her disability and became a world-class sprinter in 1960 with three gold medals. Then, there were Nadia Comaneci with seven perfect scores and three gold medals as a 14-year-old gymnast and Mark Spitz with more gold medals than any other swimmer.

TWO CONTEMPORARY OLYMPIC STORIES

Did you ever wonder what drives individuals to seek the gold, what happens to gold medal winners in the rest of their lives, or how they used their skills as an Olympian to continue their personal growth? And, what of those Olympians who didn't finish first—are they "losers"?

Here are personal insights from two Olympians who are not household names. Pat McCormick accomplished her feats in 1952 and 1956, long before television emerged as a celebrity-maker. Vince Poscente, Canada's fastest speed skier with a record 135 mph, was a contender in the 1992 Winter Olympics.

Pat McCormick is a success, as her curriculum vitae clearly shows. But the lessons to be learned from Pat aren't listed there. Like many over-achievers, she encountered adversity first and learned from it. While she began swimming and diving early in life, she didn't know anything about the Olympics until she was 14 years old.

Training for the Olympic trials in 1948, Pat missed being on the three-woman team by 1/100th of a point. That, Pat tells us, was her motivation.

"When I missed by 1/100th of a point, it was as if a light came on," Pat says. While she was crying at her misfortune, she decided she would not only qualify for the 1952 Olympics, she would win a gold medal.

"Then I thought," says Pat, "why not go for two Olympics and win four gold medals?"

So she began training the next day for what she told us was her "magnificent obsession." The people who knew her well knew that she had what it would take to achieve. We asked Pat this year, 1995, what her secrets were. She said there are no secrets, but her formula for success is this: "First, you must have a dream. Second, you've got to work. Third, you have to develop a high-failure quotient—not being afraid to fail. Fourth, you need to surround yourself with winners. And, finally, you should continue stepping up from the victory stand," says Pat.

Pat McCormick had a big dream to do something no other person had ever done. But she knew the dream, while necessary, wasn't sufficient. Those who knew her best at that time said she just outworked the other divers.

Today, she says her work ethic, combined with her message that it's OK to fail, are what inspire audiences around the world. She admits that learning how to fail wasn't easy, but she not only didn't allow failure to get in her way, she used it as motivation to achieve.

We asked Pat about mistakes she had made along the way and replied, "You should surround yourself with greatness, with winners, with good coaches, and with loved ones. There were times when I wasn't growing and, more often than not, I didn't have the right coaches for me at that time."

Well, Pat did it right. She won two medals in 1952 (the first year since 1912 that the Soviet Union competed), and then set her sights on 1956, but not before meeting two other challenges along the way. When the 1952 Olympics were over, she felt "empty." The Olympics were exhilarating for Pat, and coming down from the "high" wasn't easy. She believes that in diving, as in any form of life's work, a support system is needed. She really needed such a support system when one "small complication" presented itself; Pat was pregnant and due to deliver only five months before the 1956 Olympic trials.

Her coach then was her husband, and together they made it through. Pat McCormick believes that "if you really want something, you can have it." And have it she did. She not only made the team, she won her third gold medal. And, when she found herself in second place going into her last dive in the 10-meter platform event, Pat put her "magnificent obsession" on the line. Here's how one writer, John Weyler of the *Los Angeles Times*, described the scene: "She stood ready, looking outwardly calm. The crowd was silent. Pat stepped forward, ran, hurled, took off and was so high that she seemed to hang suspended over the tower before spinning and twisting through an almost perfect dive for a score of 18.17 points."

That dive gave her first place, her double-double, and a place in history.

THE YAHOO THEORY

Vince Poscente has a different story. Vince Poscente was a finalist in the 1992 Olympic Winter Games in Albertville, France. He is Canada's fastest skier with a downhill record of 135 mph. Vince is a five-time Canadian record holder in speed-skiing. Unlike Pat McCormick, he didn't get an early start. Vince didn't start competing until age 25. Why?

He follows the Yahoo theory: "If that Yahoo can do it, so can I." And he did. He trained for four years. That's not a very long time as far as Olympic training goes, but Vince was intense. He practiced hard and, in addition, did what his competition did not do—spent two hours every day visualizing and imaging. Vince became obsessed by it and eventually made the Canadian Olympic team.

Vince was one of 80 skiers vying for Olympic medals in speed-skiing. After round one he made the cut as the 20 slowest were left out. In rounds two and three he also survived the cut. After the first run in the final round Vince was in sixth place. The competitors' times were so closely packed that the difference between sixth and first place was the length of a No. 2 pencil.

"I'll never forget the feeling" as he prepared for his last run for the gold, said Vince. Out of the starting gate with his breath as obvious as a cloud in the sky, he hurtled straight downhill. This was speed-skiing—no turns, no gates, just putting skis in the fall line and letting 'em run.

At 140 mph, with adrenaline flowing and his heart pumping like a piston, the unthinkable happened—he caught an edge. Miraculously, he didn't fall, but it was enough to cost him a medal. He finished fifteenth. Was he disappointed? Yes. But Vince Poscente has no regrets. He focused on a dream of being an Olympian, of winning a medal. What he realizes today is that it is the process, the discipline, and the spirit of the Olympics that is all-important. He wasn't a medalist, but his achievements are nonetheless as impressive.

Like Pat McCormick, Vince Poscente is a speaker who shares an inspiring message with his audiences. They have been there. Both achieved more than most people can ever imagine. But in the daily game of life, they know that the process of growth and of achieving never ends.

The Olympic Creed formed by Pierre de Coubertin puts it all in perspective: "The most important thing at the Olympic Games is not to win but to take part, just as the most important thing in life is not to triumph but the struggle. The essential thing is not to have conquered but to have fought well."

17

HELPING PEOPLE GROW™

by Jim Cathcart

Founder of Cathcart Institute of La Jolla, California. An international speaker and author on growth strategies, Jim Cathcart has delivered over 2,000 presentations worldwide during over 22 years as a professional speaker. He is the author of twelve books, including *Relationship Selling* and *The Acorn Principle*. A past president of the National Speakers Association, his emphasis is on helping people know themselves and grow themselves. Phone: 800-222-4883; e-mail:Info@cathcart.com; web site: www.cathcart.com.

W hether you are a coach, a parent, a manager or an entrepreneur, you are charged with the need to develop people. In order to help people grow, two things will always be needed: education and motivation. Education must be continual and motivation must be renewed daily.

What you know and what you do are the two things that determine the direction and quality of your life. Your relationships, your career, and even your health will always reflect what you know (your awareness) and what you do (your behavior). The good news is that both of those areas are within your control. You can increase what you know through various forms of education. What you do can be improved through various forms of motivation.

This chapter will show you a way to assess yourself and others in any context to determine how to attain better and greater achievement, while at the same time producing peace of mind. The model I call the Mastery Grid displays the four most common modes in which people operate, their patterns of performance related to their awareness and their behavior.

Olympic performers in all fields have known for years that these two variables hold the key to high achievement and deep personal satisfaction.

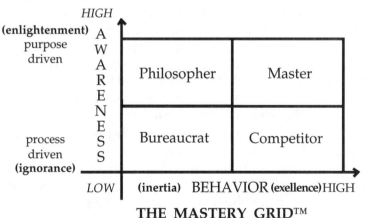

THE MASTERY GRID™

AWARENESS

Let's examine the vertical scale measuring "Awareness" first. Awareness on this scale ranges from ignorance to enlightenment. The higher part of the scale is labeled "purpose-driven" and the lower part "process-driven." Generally speaking, the more you know, the more connections you see and the better you understand the purposes behind things. The less you know the more your focus is merely on the processes.

For example: If you are familiar with computers and the language they use, then the tasks, "saving your documents," "cutting and pasting," or doing a "group replace" are simple and purposeful. You not only can perform the functions, you also understand *why* they need to be done.

If computers are not familiar to you, then you'd simply notice what happens (the process) without having a clue as to why the computer is behaving in a particular way. "Hey, my computer screen is blinking. What does that mean?"

The same holds true with people. The better we know them, the more we understand why they think and act as they do. The less we know them, the more we simply notice their behavior. This applies to specific individuals and also to people in general. The more we understand one person, the more likely we will be to understand others.

So, to know more…notice more. Pay attention to all the messages people convey, not just to their words. Start making finer distinctions in all that you encounter; people, situations, relationships, systems, etc. Notice more and soon you'll see patterns emerge. Patterns which can teach you what to do next. Patterns which hold the key to getting the results you want. The more you know, the more options you'll see…and the better the odds will be in your favor.

I like to ride motorcycles, always have. My current bike is the fifth one I've owned. But years ago when I knew very little about how motorcycles worked my new bike suddenly stalled on the ride home from the dealership. I called the dealer and he walked me through a problem diagnosis over the phone. In a moment the problem was solved and I was on my way again. What had happened? The fuel was not reaching the engine because a switch was turned off. How embarrassing!

Because I didn't know much about the machine all I could say was "It suddenly died." But the dealer's mind immediately began to analyze the problem by category: Is it getting electricity? Is it getting fuel? Is a vital part broken? The dealer had a much higher awareness of the machine than I did.

HOW TO THINK

The hardest part about dealing with any situation is determining how to think about it. Einstein said that was the biggest challenge in discovering the theory of relativity. Once he decided how to think about it, the answers he sought materialized quickly and easily.

The more you know, the more options you'll see. And the better you'll understand the principles at work behind the circumstances. Ralph Waldo Emerson said, "If you learn only methods, you'll be tied to your methods. But if you'll learn *principles*, you can devise your own methods."

This applies to your job, your physical challenges and to your life in general. This essay describes a way of thinking about the principles of human behavior and how they relate to achieving Olympic mastery in anything you do.

BEHAVIOR

If we plotted behavior on a horizontal scale it would range from inertia (no action) to excellence (world-changing performance).

The left half of the scale represents doing only what is necessary. The right half represents doing more than is required. Most people do not exceed requirements. They could, but they usually don't. Doing what they are paid to do and no more is normal to them. These people preserve the status quo. Because they do only what is required, things tend to stay the same.

A smaller group of people seem regularly to do more than they have to do. They exceed their employer's, friend's or customer's expectations in all situations. They give more than is required and overfill their space. These are the producers who add energy to the advancement of organizations and projects. These are the givers who go beyond the call of duty and take initiative. They add that extra touch that makes all the difference. They not only serve, they "up-serve." They give more than they have to.

When it comes time for raises or bonuses, which one do you think deserves the money? The giver, of course. But in recent years much of society has adopted the pattern of only doing what is necessary. Rarely do people put in extra hours unless they're sure they'll get overtime pay. And since lawsuits are so commonplace almost no one wants to take bold initiative. They frequently chant, "I'm not paid to do extra work,"...and they never will be.

The reason people should regularly give more than they are expected to is because giving is the joy in life. Giving more than is required creates a purpose bigger than ourselves. Life only advances when someone does more than he or she is required to do.

You never hear people say that they had a fulfilling and satisfying life because they always beat their competitors and netted a high return on their money. A satisfying life comes about in relation to serving other people and making human connections. Money is an abstract measure of how much value you are giving to the world. The road to peace of mind, deep satisfaction and greater self-respect is the road taken when someone does more than he or she is required to do.

What we're talking about here is making a difference in the world. Starting with right where you are.

How and why

Now combine the scale of awareness with the scale of behavior: Knowing and Doing. Consider awareness: The less you know, the fewer options you see. The less you know, the more you focus only on functions or processes. For example, if you are new on a job, you will likely first learn only processes. "This form goes here. Lunch break is at 11:45. All employees park in the remote lot." But if you seek to understand why things are done as they are, things will take on a whole new meaning for you. The more you know the more you see purposes behind the processes, the whys behind the hows. "This form goes here *because* everyone needs access to it. Lunch is at 11:45

because it allows us to beat the crowds at the cafeteria. The remote parking lot is used *because* it is free to employees."

Until you understand the reasons behind things, you can't make decisions. You are unable to lead or exert initiative because you don't have the one type of information required by all leaders everywhere: an understanding of the *purpose* of the activity, the desired end result. Without clarity of purpose, as you try to be productive, you are limited to only the simplest of tasks. This forces you to behave as a bureaucrat; you make almost no decisions and exert no initiative. You are, in fact, process driven.

To be more productive, new knowledge is essential. This leads us back to the awareness scale. When you teach people why things are done in a certain way, you vastly broaden their understanding. The person who knows how may have a job, but the person who knows *why* will be his boss. When one understands why then he can see more than one way to get there. A person, employee, can make more decisions and adjust to changes that arise, and still reach a goal. This person is more likely to give more to each task. A purpose provides a motive which manifests itself as motivation.

PRINCIPLES, PURPOSES AND PEOPLE

In the old world of management, withholding information was a way for management to retain control. Today, that is the quickest way for managers to become obsolete. The easiest way to manage people today is to give them as much awareness as possible. If they know why they are doing things, then even if they make mistakes, they fall forward toward the goal. The more they understand, the less supervision they need. And vice versa. People who have no larger goals or don't know the purposes behind their tasks require your constant supervision. The same is true in raising children. If you teach them purposes and principles, they become more capable of acting without constant supervision.

In the once-popular TV action series, "McGuyver," the lead character always saved the day by devising some amazing contraption from the most common materials. He was able to do this because he understood the basic *principles* of physics, biology and chemistry which applied to all situations.

Principles explain why things function as they do. As Emerson said, "If you learn the principles...you can devise your own methods." A Why always overrules a How.

The awareness continuum flows like this from high to low: The *Purpose* selects the *Principles* which apply and the *Principles* select the *Processes*. For example: If you want to achieve Olympic-level competence in a sport, your behavior will need to be very different from those who simply seek to win their next competition. Your higher purpose of shooting for the Olympic level causes you to see how knowledge and skill must constantly grow. It would not be enough to just win a match. You would want to use each competition to sharpen your skills and train yourself for even higher levels of performance. You would be competing more with your own prior performance than with the performance of others. You'd be seeking to master the principles of peak performance and you'd follow the processes that took you there.

The less you know of purposes and principles, the less you are worth to a business and the easier it is to replace you. The more you know, the more you are worth and the harder you are to replace. I recall the story of one manager whose recent mistake had lost his firm over $100,000. He reported the error to the company president and said, "I suppose I'm fired." The president said, "Heck no you're not fired! I just spent an extra $100,000 to train you. I can't afford to lose you right now." That's assuming he learned a great deal from his mistake. But I think you get the point.

MOTIVATION AND THE MINIMUM

Refer to the behavior scale once again. As long as one only meets requirements, the status quo persists. Things only advance when someone does more than he or she is "paid" to do. Minimal performance equals no advancement. Exceptional performance equals growth.

This can be as simple an action as straightening up your room when you're an overnight guest or filling up the tank in a borrowed car. It can also be going the extra mile for a customer or completing an assignment ahead of schedule and under budget. It means continuing to practice long after you feel you understand what you are doing.

Every time someone does more than is required, the world advances and things improve.

This scale indicates the quantity of productive effort one puts into the task. The higher an individual charts on the behavior scale, the less motivation that individual requires.

Awareness relates to Quality as Behavior relates to Quantity. Where the awareness scale shows how much supervision one requires, the behavior scale shows how much motivation is needed.

Now when I say "motivation" I don't mean superficial incentives. I mean helping individuals discover their motives for increasing their output. If they have no motives, there will be no motivation. So study the individual (or yourself) to understand what would cause him or her to want to exceed requirements.

Part of this solution comes from reinforcing the attitude that exceptional performance should be the norm. When I do seminars on Customer Service, my primary emphasis is not on what to do but rather on how to get people to want to do more than they have to do. That's where the most value is found.

Look back at the behavior scale. Those who simply meet requirements are the most unhappy and least satisfied. They know that their contribution is minimal. Because of that, they have less self-respect and more problems. They get ill more often, miss work, experience severe mood swings and earn little praise. This leads them to become somewhat paranoid and defensive. They blame circumstances for their problems. They "had a bad day" or "were just unlucky" and, "it's not fair."

They memorize the employment policies and labor laws that justify their "victim" posture and they demand more benefits and privileges. Since things aren't getting better for them, they assume someone else must be responsible for their dilemma. They complain of the work load and lack of management support.

To solve their problems and allay their fears all they really need to do is to pay better attention and increase their performance. The minute they start giving more, they get more praise, productivity, and privileges in return. People who give more, respect themselves more and everything around them begins to improve. My friend, Steve Curtis, says that the formula for success is: Show up, pay attention, tell the truth and release the outcome (let things happen naturally, don't push). I would add only: Do your part, and then some.

We have now created a grid with four quadrants. Low awareness and low behavior, high awareness and low behavior, low awareness and high behavior, and high awareness with high behavior.

When both your awareness and your behavior are low you operate as a Bureaucrat. The focus is on performing functions and meeting requirements. Both purpose and growth become lower priorities. This is the lower left corner of the grid. When people operate in this Bureaucrat state they need two things in order to grow: more awareness and improved performance. Educate them and motivate them. For far too long we've thought of jobs instead of roles. A job is usually defined as a limited set of tasks or responsibilities. Whereas a role implies your interdependence with others. If your role is to bring in new business, then your job is more than just making a sale. If your role is to lead your department, then your job is more than just managing things and supervising people.

When one understands his or her role in any situation, he begins to see purposes behind the processes, leading to a reason or motive to do more than is required.

In the upper left of our grid is high awareness and low behavior. Someone in this category knows why things are done and recognizes the purpose behind the processes. The trouble is, although this person knows quite a bit, he or she seldom acts on this knowledge. The behavior remains within the minimum requirements. I call this the Philosopher mode. These people have more awareness than the Bureaucrat but about the same level of performance.

These are the people who talk a great game but seldom play. They often become intellectually arrogant and cynical. Because they understand a lot, they feel above the need to do more. It's as if exceeding what is required would somehow lower their superior status.

My friend Brian Tracy calls these people the "Articulate Incompetents." They could do more, they just don't. What these

Philosopher types need most is to act on their intellect, to put their knowledge into action. Until they hold themselves to a higher standard of behavior, they will remain lonely and aloof. They can't think themselves out of this mode, it requires action and lots of it. They must break their inertia through disciplined self-motivation. Do more and start to grow. They have the education but still need the motivation.

The lower right quadrant is low awareness and high behavior. This is where plenty of exceptional action is taken but the focus is mostly on doing, not on the reasons for doing them. This is the mode called Competitor.

Competitors are focused on winning only. Their drive is simply to be first, best, biggest, most or somehow to outdistance those around them. They adopt Vince Lombardi's famous line, "Winning isn't everything, it's the only thing." The assumption of the Competitor is that somewhere out on the exceptional behavior continuum they will "win" and can then relax and savor their victory.

The irony is, it doesn't work that way. Success is not a moment in time, it is a state of being. It is when the material rewards and the inner satisfaction occur simultaneously. Achievement without purpose cannot produce fulfillment.

What Competitors really need is a greater sense of purpose. They need for their "wins" to have more meaning and value. This requires an increase in their awareness, more education, deeper thinking. They must understand the bigger picture in order to give meaning to their efforts. They need deeper motives behind the motivation.

Sometimes when we refocus on our higher purpose it makes competing almost irrelevant. For example: In the mid-1980s, Harley Davidson Motorcycle Company changed its operation from a manufacturing-focus (producing motorcycles) to a customer-focus (satisfying people's wants) operation. The company asked customers and potential customers what they liked and what they wanted, then retooled the entire company to produce it for them. They even formed a club of Harley Owners to help them stay closely in touch with their market base. This resulted in Harley Davidson's worldwide dominance of the market for big cruiser bikes for years. Today,

Harley Davidson has more demand than it can satisfy. For almost 10 years its competition had literally become irrelevant. If a person wants a Harley, a substitute just won't do. When Harley Davidson took its already high behavior and added to it a bigger purpose, they mastered their marketplace.

The upper right quadrant is high awareness and high behavior. I call this Mastery. At this level the person is purpose driven and exceeds requirements. The individual is a contributor and makes a difference. Consequently, this person is also a leader, whether the position reflects it or not. The Master needs neither more education nor more motivation because he or she is constantly generating both. What is needed is simply support and empowerment. This is the only quadrant where a person gains a sense of fulfillment. The life and the work of the Master produces the most satisfaction.

All people desire a satisfying life, a life they can be proud of, and with a clear sense of purpose, coupled with exceptional output, they can create such a life. To sustain Mastery, all one needs is to grow constantly in awareness and continually give more than is required.

Masters have a natural glow about them. Others want to be around them. Their charisma is magnetic. It's not that they are necessarily charming or witty, it's just that their self-assurance and generosity appeals to everyone.

Look at the grid now. Where have you been operating lately? High or low awareness? High or low behavior? Whichever it has been, you can change it for the better by following my two maxims:

> To know more...notice more and, to have more...give more. There is always plenty of motivation when you know your own motives fully.

18

FOCUS, TEAMWORK & COMMITMENT

by Jim Clack

Jim Clack is a 13-year veteran NFL lineman, an all-pro, and a recipient of two Super Bowl rings. He was a star performer for the Super Bowl champion Pittsburgh Steelers for nine years and then captain of the New York Giants for another four years. A graduate of Wake Forest University, Jim's unique background includes a full range of business experiences as a corporate officer, speaker and consultant. His clients include Isuzu Trucks, Hardee's Food Systems, Sara Lee, The Executive Committee, Becton Dickinson, Amerlink and others. Phone: 800-633-7762 / 910-282-6303 Sales@ Brooksgroup.com.

If I learned anything during a very fulfilling 13-year career in the National Football League it was simply this: Focus, Teamwork and Commitment are the most necessary components to individual and team success. I am confident that the very same formula is essential for Olympic success. I am even more confident that they are the success components in the real world of business and personal growth.

In 1969 I graduated from college with a promising professional football career ahead of me. I had been a High School All-American selection, had more than 150 scholarship offers and had enjoyed a relatively successful college career. It was good enough, I was sure, to get into the NFL as a modestly high draft choice.

Draft day came…and went, no draft, no call and no interest from any NFL team. I was despondent beyond belief. I had suffered the first real failure and indignity of my life.

Several days following the draft I did receive a call from the newly appointed (and very young, I might add) head coach of the then floundering Pittsburgh Steelers.

"Hello, Jim. My name is Chuck Noll. I have just been appointed as head coach of the Pittsburgh Steelers. How would you like to be a Steeler?" The phone call of my life had been made!

I can remember it like it was yesterday. I didn't care what they paid me, when I was to be paid or even what position they wanted me to play. But I was going to achieve my dream—too play on an NFL Team. But it wasn't going to be that easy.

For one thing, I was an undersized lineman. I finished my senior year at Wake Forest weighing 215 pounds. Coach Noll told me to report at 240. Gaining 25 pounds as a 22 year old was a lot harder than it is now, some quarter of a century later!

But I did it, as well as a lot more things they asked me to do. Preseason camp was tough, much tougher than I thought it would be.

The greatest fear that permeates any professional football camp is not the heat, nor the tough conditioning. It's not even the wrath of the veterans on the rookies. Instead, it is the "Turk." No, the "Turk" is not a Middle Eastern immigrant. It's the dread of being cut.

Here's how it was done at the Steeler's camp. Players would report to the locker room daily, including the day of cuts. On those fateful days of paring down the roster, you would go to your locker and open it up—to see if your equipment had been cleaned out.

Yes, cleaned out: No equipment meant no tomorrow with the Steelers. In fact, an empty locker meant not even a today. You were cut. Eliminated. Fired. Gone. With no questions asked.

Through hard work, discipline and maybe even a little luck I made it through the first phase of preseason camp. Undersized, not drafted, and awarded a whopping $500 signing bonus that wouldn't even buy a pair of shoes for today's highly paid athletes, I made it through the camp…until the very last day when the last cut was to be executed. My last hurdle. I went to the locker room with a sense of positive expectancy, fully expecting to become a Pittsburgh Steeler. I carefully and hesitantly opened my locker, expecting to get dressed for practice, only to discover that my harshest nightmare had come true. It was cleaned out! It was as clean as if nothing had ever been in it. Every trace of my equipment was gone, along with my dream of professional football.

Everything I had worked for throughout my entire athletic career was gone in the flash of an eye. But I immediately had an idea and a compelling reaction.

I knew I could gain weight, stay in shape and come back. I know Coach Noll would give me that chance. And he did.

He made a suggestion I couldn't refuse and I soon found myself in Norfolk, Virginia, playing semiprofessional football for the Norfolk Neptunes of the Continental League.

It certainly wasn't the NFL and the Neptunes were a far cry from the Steelers. But I still had a chance. My dream was still alive, but only if I maintained my *focus*.

And focus I did. I slept, ate, breathed and lived Neptune football. And Neptune football would become Steeler football.

I reported to camp in 1970 in the best shape of my life. I had spent the entire year focused on one thing: making the Pittsburgh Steelers as an offensive lineman.

I maintained my focus. At daily workout sessions in the gym, I drove myself until I dropped, often to the point of tears. More times than I can remember I almost passed out from exhaustion.

This time I knew what to expect. I knew the ropes. I would make it this time. And I did…to the very last day of camp.

Once again, I went to the locker room, opened the locker and peered in. I was even more positive this time that I had done all I could to make the squad and that my hard work and off-season effort would pay off for me.

I gazed into my locker. At first I couldn't believe it. But the reality hit me. It was empty, as empty as a toy store on Christmas morning. But not nearly as empty as the feeling in my stomach—I actually felt ill. Life wasn't fair. Football wasn't fair.

I had worked myself to the bone for two solid years, done everything asked of me and more. Was this how effort was to be rewarded ? Life had to be more fair than this, didn't it?

There are a lot more Olympic hopefuls who *don't* make their Olympic teams than do. There are a lot more also-rans than champions. And I felt like a real also-ran. More strongly, I felt as if I had wasted two years of my life on a dream. And that dream had robbed me. Have you ever felt like that?

In retrospect, things did work out well for me that year as I was placed on the Steeler Taxi Squad and supplemented my meager income by being a substitute teacher. I worked as hard as anyone who actually suited up to play on Sunday, even though I knew I was just a practice player. In actuality, I was a blocking dummy for the "real" Steelers.

An interesting question: What got me there? What led me eventually to become a real Steeler? I am convinced that it was nothing more than my almost maniacal commitment to *focus*, and staying focused on one thing—my elusive dream. Nothing distracted me: not adversity, lost time, pain, exhaustion, the anguish of failure—nothing.

Olympic champions are like that. Business and professional champions are like that. I believe that life's champions are like that. Pure, dogged and determined focus can compensate for a lack of talent, physical inability or just about anything else.

THE POWER OF TEAMWORK

The next year I became a part of the Team. But learning Teamwork was another big obstacle, particularly since the team I was to become a part of had experienced a dismal season the previous year. In fact, we were to have just as miserable a season in my first full season as a Steeler in 1971.

We struggled for several more seasons and lost a lot more games than we won. But we were going to make our mark in the NFL. We had a couple of advantages. What were they? Here they are:

- An owner committed to being successful (Art Rooney);
- A head coach committed to excellence (Chuck Noll);
- A solid success system (our offensive and defensive schemes);
- Marvelously skilled position coaches (line, backs, etc.);
- Players who were hungry to win (47 of us who were tired of losing).

It sounds like a successful business, doesn't it? Some call it synergy. Others call it organizational effectiveness. I have a simpler term for it: Teamwork.

Teamwork occurs when all people work together and none of them really care about who gets the credit, or who gets the blame. Everyone is working together to achieve the same thing. For us, it was the Superbowl.

For Olympians it is a gold medal. For sales organizations it may be market share or market dominance. For manufacturing organizations it could be a certain level of quality, a better yield or reduced expenses.

The point is that a clearly focused effort coupled with the power of teamwork is an unstoppable combination.

In our case, the team became the single most dominant force in many of our lives. We were totally committed to the Black and Gold, absolutely, 100 percent Pittsburgh Steelers. Everyone, from the owner to the ball boy, from the coaches to the ticket takers, was completely dedicated.

Our fans (some may call them our customers) also got into the act. The "Terrible Towels" and "Gerela's Gorillas" (named after our marvelous kicker, Roy Gerela) became symbols of our team and Three Rivers Stadium.

Most important, we knew we had total commitment from the top. Our owner, Art Rooney was absolutely devoted to one thing: having the best team he could put together. He selected and supported the coaching staff. Our training and equipment staffs were committed to the team. The players were committed to the team.

Today, as I work with organizations around the world I do my best to communicate to them that Teamwork is not just a "player thing." Rather, it is the amalgamation of the efforts of everyone who is part of that organization.

As Olympians march into the stadium on opening day of the Olympics, there is much more to the team than just the athletes. Also on the team are parents, sponsors, boosters, coaches, trainers, administrators, nutritionists, maintenance people and a lot more. The players merely represent the Team.

THE PASSION OF COMMITMENT

After a 13-year career in which I played on two Superbowl teams, served as team captain, was named to several All-Star teams and was even nominated as NFL Man-Of-The-Year for Charity Work, I retired with a sense of enthusiasm for my next career.

I was confident that my career as an NFL player had prepared me for anything that would occur in my life—good or bad. But I was not prepared for what happened on the evening of July 17, 1985. My wife leisurely pulled our car onto a lonely highway after we had been out to dinner one evening.

Bearing down on us was a huge, 18-wheeler, fully loaded, and moving at 60 plus miles per hour. We never saw it coming. He never saw us, until it was too late. We were completely crushed. Miraculously, my wife survived. Since the truck hit my side of the car at full speed, it was even more miraculous that I survived. It took two hours for me to be cut from the wreckage. I had more injuries than could be counted. A fractured pelvis, a broken back, a ruptured spleen, a severed tongue, a broken leg—these were only half of my injuries.

I was unconscious for three solid weeks. When I awoke, I had no idea where I was or even why I was there. My first explanation came from a neurosurgeon who was tugging on my leg. He subsequently informed me that I had been in the accident a full three weeks prior!

Doctors told me that my recovery would be slow, painful, arduous and even questionable. At one point, my family was told that my chances for recovery were slim to none. They were even told to visit me and say their farewells. In all, I spent 17 more days in intensive care and another six months in rehabilitation.

It was through all of this that I learned the most powerful lesson of all. Yes, I knew that focus is critical and teamwork essential. But without total commitment, nothing else matters.

I committed myself to the biggest challenge of my life. Because of concentrated focus and a great team comprised of my family, friends, doctors and other medical personnel, I was able to recover fully and regain a good percentage of my previous physical capacities.

Without their full and uncompromising commitment I wouldn't be here today. Without my personal commitment to therapy and rehabilitation I wouldn't be writing this chapter. Without my complete commitment to struggle and survival, I wouldn't even be alive today.

The underlying principle is this: Total dedication (commitment) by a group of people (a team) to a clear goal (focus) is what determines ultimate success.

Olympic athletes understand this. World class athletes in any sport understand it. Successful business organizations understand it. What is essential is that individuals understand its application in their own lives. It is really a simple formula for success, one that proves itself day after day in a variety of settings: sometimes in life or death situations and sometimes just in games.

The magic of focus coupled with the power of teamwork fueled by the passion of commitment will accelerate performance. I invite you to master this formula for your own success. But you can't do it alone. And you can't accomplish it without a clear focus, and I guarantee you can't do it without commitment. Win your own Olympic Game of Life and step into your own Winner's Circle.

19

THE SPECIAL OLYMPIAN

by Dennis Mannering, C.S.P.

Dennis Mannering has made more than 2,500 presentations during his career as a professional speaker. He has acquired the reputation as the "Guru of Common Sense" in customer service, leadership, teamwork and sales. He gets to the heart of quality living and working as he provides general, and on-going, training to competitive businesses. Phone: 920-339-0011; e-mail: Dmannering@aol. com; web site: www.members.aol.com/Mannerings.

In 1956, I left the farm in Missouri to live with an older brother in upstate New York. At that time, he and his wife had two daughters and lived in an apartment over a hardware store.

In the fall of that year, there was exciting news. My brother and sister-in-law were expecting another child. Three children in less than four years might seem like a burden for some, but my brother thought this might be the son he had wanted so much.

He began dreaming of the son who would follow in his footsteps as a golden gloves boxing champion. Or maybe he would be a star baseball player like his grandfather. Or perhaps he would make his own mark as a football player, or basketball superstar.

*   *   *

On a cold December day, when my brother was out of town because of his work, my sister-in-law calmly asked me to call her parents because it was time for her to go to the hospital. My brother, in Pennsylvania at the time, was expected home in a day or two. But a snowstorm hit and his arrival was delayed for another day.

By the time he got home, their son Steve had been born. As my brother and I left for the hospital to see his one-day-old child, our excitement was high. Visions of Steve playing football and baseball, becoming a lawyer or a doctor, were running through our minds. Although not yet 15 years old, I shared the excitement with my brother. I dreamed of teaching my little nephew everything I knew about sports. I wanted to be his hero!

Shock and disappointment, however, were just around the corner. When we arrived at the hospital, we were told that Steve had been placed in an oxygen tent. He wasn't getting enough oxygen to his brain. Our worst fears were confirmed when the doctor told us his mental growth would be retarded. Retarded! An awful word to hear anytime, but especially so in the Fifties, when society still shunned, and sometimes shut away, those "special people"!

But we were to learn over the next 35 years what a blessing Steve would be for our family. A challenge for his parents at times, to be sure, but a joy and blessing as well.

*   *   *

I continued to live with my brother for another year before moving into a separate apartment with my mother and young sister. Steve now had a younger sister and the house my brother had purchased was quickly filling up. Although I lived within an hour's drive, I didn't see much of Steve for the next four years.

In 1961, I moved back in with my brother (to save money while attending college) and shared a room with Steve. These were the times when the "specialness" in Steve came out. That year his little brother was born and he was so proud. Steve always stood guard over his little "Marky," making sure he was fed and cared for "properly."

* * *

The following year it was time for Steve to start kindergarten. Since his test scores were lower than those of "normal" children, he was placed in a classroom with other "trainable" children. Steve could learn, but in those days in New York, not much distinction was made between different degrees of retardation so all those who were retarded to any extent were grouped together.

His parents were told he couldn't learn. Yet one evening, he stood in front of the mirror in our bedroom and recited the Pledge of Allegiance and the school prayer. Excitedly I said, "Steve, you know the Pledge of Allegiance and the school prayer.... you know it! They don't think you know it!"

"Yeah, Uncle Dennis, that's why I doh-don't do it for them," he replied. "They think I'm stupid."

Already he was teaching me about the concept of "getting what we expect." So often, the results we get from others depend on our expectations of them.

* * *

I soon moved out, got married, and started my own family. Each time I saw Steve over the years, I would be inspired. He could do so much, but people still expected so little. His honesty was more evident than his tact, a characteristic part of his "specialness." If I were to ask him if he liked my tie, he would tell the truth. Perhaps he wasn't diplomatic, but I always knew just what he was thinking.

Steve was perceptive, too. He always seemed to know if something was wrong in my life, or if I wasn't feeling good. He'd give me a little hug or a pat on the back to let me know things would be okay.

*   *   *

The moment I was proudest of Steve was in 1988, when he participated in the International Special Olympics. By this time, Steve was living in a group home and had become somewhat of a role model and leader for his roommates. His self-esteem was thriving and his confidence had increased immensely.

My brother told me that Steve had predicted he would win three gold medals. His expectations had been buoyed by his great success in the New York Special Olympics, where he won first place in three events: the softball throw, the 100-meter dash and the broad jump.

Steve began the International Special Olympics in great style. He won a gold medal in his first event: the softball throw. As I watched the video tape with tears in my eyes, I saw him standing on the first-place platform reciting the Pledge of Allegiance while the Stars and Stripes were raised and the national anthem played.

*   *   *

That was the only gold medal he won. But he did win a silver and a bronze in his last two events—three events, three medals—not bad. His coaches said he never took them off, throughout the entire week, not even when he showered.

When he got home his mom and dad were waiting for him at the airport. Then and only then did he take off his medals. He gave the gold medal to his dad and the silver medal to his mom. He then asked where Marky was. He wanted to give his last medal, the bronze, to his little brother. Steve wanted to share his victories with his family, whom he loved dearly.

Steve has since told me, if he ever wins another medal, he'll give it to me since I "really need it."

Amazing. All the external trappings of success and victory meant less to Steve than the opportunity to share what he had with his family. We should all be so "special."

Now, Steve no longer competes in the Olympics. Instead, he works with other Special Olympians to help them become winners. He doesn't need any more medals. He knows he's special without them. Besides, he gets an even bigger kick out of seeing someone he has helped achieve great things.

* * *

We all learned a lot from Steve that year. As a matter of fact, we've learned a lot from Steve since the day he was born. His ability to show his love has always touched us in a special way. He has taught others how to show their love, too. When "Marky" got married, he stood up at the reception to thank all those who had come to help the young couple celebrate their day. In particular, he thanked my wife and me for traveling such a long distance to be there. As he finished, he said, "I love you, Uncle Dennis and Aunt Wendy."

I was very moved by the courage it took for him to say such a thing in front of all his macho buddies, so I sought him out later to tell him how impressed and touched I was. He replied, "I wouldn't have been able to do that a few years ago, but Steve tells me he loves me all the time. He really taught me how to express my love."

A Special Olympian? You bet! As I travel the country, I meet many people who have "special" folks in their families, too. Many of them have similar stories to tell.

I share Steve with all of you who have doubts about what you can accomplish, or if you need additional inspiration to tackle a difficult problem. Steve has overcome a lot to become a special hero! You can, too.

20

OLYMPIC DREAMS

By Les Brown

Les Brown has been a full-time public speaker since 1986 when he formed, Les Brown Unlimited, Inc. a providor of motivational tapes and materials, workshops, and personal/professional development programs for individuals, companies and organizations. In 1991, his PBS program entitled "You Deserve," was awarded a Chicago-area Emmy and became a leading fund-raising program for PBS stations nationwide. He is the author of *Live!*
Phone: 800-733-4226 / 810-229-0458

From an Arkansas sharecropper's son, to an East St. Louis school girl sprinting through squalid streets, to a strapping Wisconsin lad from a family of nine, hundreds of Olympic athletes have not only lived their dreams, they have sparked our dreams too with their courage and their accomplishments. The Olympic Games are perhaps the world's greatest and most dramatic stage for those in pursuit of life-long goals and dreams. The Olympics are as much an artistic as an athletic event, for the pursuit of dreams is the art of living life as it should be lived—fully, enthusiastically, with every breath you take.

We take great inspiration from our Olympians, not just from the strength of their bodies, but from the strength of their characters. The strength of character that enabled, for example, Jesse Owens, Jackie Joyner-Kersee and Dan Jansen to endure incredible sacrifices, pain, and labor before and during their actual Olympic events is even more awesome than their incredibly tuned athletic skills and powerful physiques. We often fail to consider how many defeats these athletes had to endure before the victories began to come. How much pain preceded victory? How much sacrifice paved the way for success? It is not the Olympics that makes these individuals champions. It is the determination that brought them here that sets them apart.

100 POUNDS OF COTTON

"Everybody should have a dream," said Jesse Owens, the grandson of a slave and son of an Arkansas sharecropper. "Everybody should work toward that dream. And if you believe hard enough, whether it be in the Olympic Games, or be in the business world, or the music world or the educational world, it all comes down to one thing. One day we can all stand on the top of the victory stand, and one day we can watch our flag rise above all others to the crescendo of our national anthem. And one day, you can say, on this day, `I am a champion.'"

You have probably heard of track-star Jesse Owens, winner of four gold medals at the 1936 Olympic Games in Germany. But I'll bet that you didn't know much about his upbringing. He was only 7 years old when he was first taken into the field and ordered to pick 100 pounds of cotton a day. He knew what work was all about. And he used that knowledge, that character, to recreate himself from a field hand into a champion.

Although Jesse Owens is remembered primarily for his Olympic accomplishments, the record book shows that perhaps his greatest performance occurred in 1935 when, as an athlete at Ohio State University, he broke four world records and tied another in one afternoon. What a champion! What an accomplishment it was to come out of poverty, from a background of repression, and then to prove himself a champion to the world, in defiance of tyrant Adolph Hitler, and all others who had held you back or put you down.

POTATO CHIPS BAGS

Jackie Joyner-Kersee knows the fire that lit Jesse Owens' soul and spurred him on to greatness. It burns as strongly in her. She grew up in East St. Louis, one of the most blighted and tragic cities in America—a city that once nearly had to sell off its city hall to pay its debts. As a girl, the future world's long-jump champion went to a city park to collect sand by filling up old potato chip bags. She made trip after trip, until she had enough to fill a small pit to jump into. Winos would block off city streets for her, stopping traffic, when she trained for track events as a high school student.

Jackie Joyner-Kersee won gold medals in the long jump and the heptathlon in the 1988 Olympics. In the 1992 Olympics, she again took the gold in the heptathlon, and a bronze in the long jump. She became the first woman to win multi-event titles at two Olympics and the first athlete of either sex to win multi-event medals in three Olympics. We know from the medals around her neck that Jackie Joyner-Kersee is an Olympian. Is she a champion in life? Ask those children in her hometown, where she is now working to rebuild the youth center in that park where she gathered sand in potato chip bags for her jumping pit. Her goal is to have it built by the time the 1996 Olympics are underway.

"I remember how tough it was," she said recently about her own youth in East St. Louis, "but at the time, I didn't really realize how tough it was because of the people around me and on the team. I tell girls today, 'When resources come your way utilize them, but don't forget'."

MIAMI MAMIE

Like Joyner-Kersee, I come from very humble origins and but grew up determined to rise above the circumstances of my birth. My twin brother, Wesley, and I were abandoned as infants in a vacant building in an impoverished neighborhood in Miami. We were found and adopted by Mamie Brown, a devoted and loving woman who worked as a maid, field hand and cook to raise us on her own.

Mamie, who died only recently, had always wanted "someone in this world to love" and believe me, she worked hard to realize her dream of having a family. She taught my brother and me a great deal about working for a dream. Many times in my life I have called upon the lessons she passed on through her perseverance and hard work. I needed to.

As a boy, I was placed in classes for the educable mentally handicapped. Perhaps more than a learning disability, my problem was simply hyperactivity, but it took me many years to overcome the stigma and low self-image of being called a "special ed" student. Incidentally, I recently met another man who had dealt with a similar problem in his schooling because he had a speech impediment. That man eventually became the CEO of the Chicago public school system, where he is determined to raise the level of education for all students.

I relate my personal background not because I compare myself to an Olympian—not even on my best day. I simply want to demonstrate that regular people like you and me experience aspects of the Olympic challenge in our own lives. I want to encourage you to take a different view of these great athletes as they compete on this grand, global stage. I want you to think of the many smaller, unheralded and quiet victories that brought them to this point and consider that, while all of us may not compete on such a grand scale, we all pursue dreams. All of us have to overcome challenges along the way to becoming champions in our own right.

Perhaps the most celebrated and compelling of all recent Olympic figures is speed-skater Dan Jansen, the athletic but shy son of a West Allis, Wisconsin, police officer and his nurse wife. Dan's story is rooted in his quest for Olympic medals, but it has certainly grown larger than even the Olympics. Why? Because you and I witnessed not only his dramatic success in the 1994 games in Norway, we also witnessed his failures, repeated failures, as he went after his dream with a determination and strength of character that will serve as an inspiration for years and years to come.

A skater of legendary power, Dan was the favorite in both the 500- and 1,000-meter speed skating events in the 1988 Olympic Winter Games. He was already an Olympian, just in being there, but when it came time to compete, he was burdened with a weight beyond the strength of even an Olympic athlete.

"I'LL BE BACK"

His oldest sister, Jane, died of leukemia, just seven hours before Dan lined up for the 500-meter. Informed by the media, the world watched with its heart in its throat, as the obviously distraught Jansen fell just ten seconds into the race and was eliminated from competition. Three nights later, Dan made another courageous effort, but the grief and mental strain were just too much. Even though he got off to a strong pace in the 1,000-meter race, Dan fell again. He lost. But he was not defeated.

He put his face in his hands briefly, but looked up to tell reporters and the world, "I'll be back." No one doubted him.

If you have ever experienced the death of a loved one, you know the burden that Dan carried with him, and you can probably understand too, how it stayed with him. Most athletes have big hearts, and though strong, those hearts are just as vulnerable as yours and mine.

Four years later, Dan Jansen was still among the best speed-skaters in the world physically; but mentally, and in his heart, he had not yet healed. The pressure of the world's attention, and the memory of what had transpired in the previous Olympics, still weighed upon the dark-haired young athlete. He missed a bronze medal by a mere sixteenth of a second in the 500 meters, and skated well below his ability in the 1,000-meter event. Once more, he came up short of his dream. Defeat, however, was not something he was going to concede.

Remember Dan Jansen's failure when you find yourself stumbling en route to your dream. Call to mind the vision of him fallen and sliding haplessly on the ice with his powerful legs sprawling and useless. Understand that it happens, that life sets you up only to knock you down. And know, as Dan Jansen knows, that it is up to you to decide whether you get back up, or whether you stay down and continue to slide along the path toward that final defeat, a life unfulfilled.

History knows that Dan Jansen got back up. The world knows he came back to try again. The same fate that had tripped him up earlier handed him an opportunity. Life does that too! And he seized it. As you and I must do.

Ordinarily, Dan would have had to wait four more years to compete in the Olympics, and it might have happened that in that period, his skills could have fallen below that competitive level. But a decision by the International Olympic Committee to begin staging the winter and summer games in separate years, resulted in the staging of another Winter Olympics just two years later.

Dan Jansen prepared for these Olympic Games like they were to be his last. Instead of retiring, as some thought he might, he skated faster and harder than ever. He skated out from under the sorrow that had confused his mind and stifled his strength and skills. Prior to the 1994 Olympics in Norway, he set a world record of 35.76 seconds in the 500-meter—making him the only skater ever to break the 36-second mark.

But ol' Mister Misery was not done yet with the young man from Wisconsin. He had been heavily favored to win the short sprint race, but yet another slip resulted in a time of 36.68 seconds and an eighth-place finish. That sprint was Dan Jansen's best event. It was his strength. Everyone in the world watching the event knew it. We saw him miss that dream again. Our hearts ached for him.

Then our hearts lifted as we saw Dan Jansen line up for the 1,000-meter race. This was not his best event, not what he had long been favored to win. Even so, it has been widely noted that perhaps no other competitor in the history of the Olympic games had so many rooting for him to win.

With the sound of the starter's gun, he set out at a world-record pace, but with just 200 meters to go, he slipped slightly. He went off balance. The world gasped. Another opportunity for failure presented itself on a silver platter.

But Dan Jansen said, "No thank you, I'll take the gold!"

And he did it in world-record time!

The world will never forget Dan Jansen's victory. I hope that you will never forget his failures. Match them to your failures, because you will have failures as you strive for your dreams. Match your despair and embarrassment, to that suffered by Dan Jansen in front of a global audience. And when you pull yourself back up, feel the courage and the enormous strength of character exhibited by the young man from Wisconsin, who pulled himself back up again and again, and again.

NEW CIRCUIT

Dan is on a different circuit these days, my circuit, in fact. He is now a public speaker and in great demand. I've heard him and believe me, he speaks better than I skate. But Dan, buddy, I'm ready to put on the blades with you anytime.

And whatever you do, I'll be with the rest of the world in wishing you well because you are a champion, a man who has devoted his life to using his gifts, a man who is taking life on.

Since I became a public speaker, I have had many people congratulate me on my "gift" for communicating with people and inspiring them. Believe me, it was not a gift, or at least, it was not a gift that came out of the box fully constructed, finely tuned and ready for use. Just as the Olympians have had to sweat and train and build themselves into superb athletes and supreme competitors, I had to develop my humble gift of gab into the ability to stir the hearts and minds of large and sophisticated audiences. And just as most Olympians start on their school athletic fields and dirt tracks, I first began speaking for free, almost pushing myself onto audiences, in order to gain experience and self-confidence. I talked to grade school children, I talked to bums on park benches and pigeons on rooftops outside my window. (A few bread crumbs helped keep that particular audience in their seats.)

I trained also by watching and listening to the best public speakers I could find. And, like those people you will watch in Atlanta, I never gave up, even when the pigeons had eaten all my crumbs and flown the coop. Even when I felt like following my brother's advice and going back to the Sears store where I'd gotten a part-time job. Even when I had my car repossessed and had to sleep on the floors of friends' apartments.

But somewhere along the way, like Jesse Owens and Jackie Joyner-Kersee and Dan Jansen, I decided "It's not over until I win!" I want that to be your motto, too, and in the spirit of the Olympic Games, I want to remind you of another lesson often imparted through athletics. You are not alone. Even in your darkest moments. Even when it seems no one in the world is on your side. You are not alone.

JESSE AND LUZ

Jesse Owens could not have felt more alone than when he entered the Olympic stadium in Berlin, Germany, under the scrutiny of the very Nazi storm troopers who were about to embark on history's most infamous course. Hatred burned from their eyes.

The Nazi newspaper had labeled the Black American athletes "The Black Auxiliaries." Hitler's fanatic followers predicted joyfully that the presence of these "inferior" men signaled that the United States was a nation in decay.

In pre-Olympic propaganda, Hitler had announced "The Americans ought to be ashamed of themselves for letting their medals be won by Negroes, I myself would never shake hands with one of them."

With Hitler, Hermann Goering, Joseph Goebbels and Heinrich Himmler watching, James Cleveland "Jesse" Owens, the grandson of slaves, won his first event, the 100-meter final, with ease. The only person close to him was another Black American, future U.S. Congressman Ralph Metcalfe.

The next day, the mood was even more ominous in a stadium that had been designed as a showcase for Nazism.

Swastikas and soldiers wearing them, were everywhere.

Jesse Owens would win every event he entered in Hitler's Olympics. But it was his performance in the long-jump that many historians would later call to mind as a harbinger of the dictator's ultimate defeat.

In competition prior to the Olympics, Jesse had already set the world record for the long jump—a record that would hold for 25 years. And, with his gold medal from the sprint already in hand, he was the clear favorite also for the Olympic long-jump competition. But he was in no way the favorite of Hitler's henchmen.

When he walked onto the long jump track still in his warm-ups, Jesse loosened up and then took an easygoing practice run at the pit. To the shock of everyone, the German officials insisted on measuring that jump and recording it as a legitimate effort, and his first attempt in the qualifying round!

Rattled by their hostility, Jesse fouled on his second attempt. He had only one try left. He had to qualify for the second round, or he would be eliminated—from his best event!

Imagine yourself in that situation. Fit it to your experiences, your darkest moments of self-doubt, the times when you felt the whole world was against you, that no one cared, that your enemies were cheering for your failure.

And then, consider this true scene in the Olympics of 1936 in Hitler's Berlin, Germany:

A tall, powerfully built, blue-eyed, blond-haired German man approaches Jesse Owens as he is preparing for his crucial third attempt at the long jump. Owens eyes him as the epitome of Hitler's arrogant view of Aryan superiority.

The German extends his hand to Jesse Owens, and introduces himself, in English, as Luz Long.

"Glad to meet you," said Owens, nervously. "How are you?"

"I'm fine," came the German's response. "The question is, How are you?"

Jesse asked what he meant. Long replied that he could see something was bothering him. "You should be able to qualify with your eyes closed," the German said.

With the ice broken, the two very different men stood talking. Long confided in Owens that he did not share Hitler's belief of Aryan superiority, even if he personally looked the part. They laughed together.

Jesse relaxed. And then one of Hitler's own athletes offered a tip. Since the qualifying distance was only 23 feet, 5 1/2 inches, why didn't Owens make a mark several inches in front of the takeoff board and jump from there to play it safe. After all, his world record in the event was 26 feet, 8 1/4 inches.

Owens thanked the German, and took his advice. He qualified on his third jump. In the finals that afternoon, Owens started out by setting an Olympic record on his first jump. On his second jump, he bettered it by 4 1/2 inches.

By this time, the story of the friendship between Luz Long and Jesse Owens had swept through the Olympic stadium. And so, the crowd of nearly 70,000 went wild, when the German matched Owens' second jump exactly.

Inspired, Owens leaped 26 feet, 5 1/2 inches on his final attempt to clinch the second of his eventual four gold medals.

And the first person who congratulated him after that long jump victory was Luz Long.

"You can melt down all the medals and cups I have," Owens wrote years later, "and they wouldn't be a plating on the 24-carat friendship I felt for Luz Long at that moment."

Live your dreams and whether you achieve them or not, you will be a champion. And know, that even in the darkest of times, you are not alone.

This is Mamie Brown's baby boy saying victory can be yours!